THE YOUNG LOUIS XIV

Borgo Press Books by ALEXANDRE DUMAS

THE YOUNG LOUIS XIV

A PLAY IN FIVE ACTS

ALEXANDRE DUMAS

Adapted and Translated by Frank J. Morlock

THE BORGO PRESS
MMXII

THE YOUNG LOUIS XIV

DEDICATION

To Conrad—yet another project that would never have come to fruition without your encouragement and support.

CONTENTS

CAST OF CHARACTERS

King Louis XIV

The Duke d'Anjou (Monsieur), aka Anjou, brother of the king

Charles Stuart (later King Charles II of England)

Mazarin

Molière

Jean Poquelin

Guitaut, Captain of the Guards

Bouchavannes, a musketeer

Count de Guiche

Marquis de Montglat

Duke de Grammont

Count de Dangeau

Duke de Villeroi

Duke de Villequier

Lyonne

Le Tellier

Superintendent Fouquet

Pimentel, the Spanish Ambassador

Guenaud, a doctor

Bernouin, Cardinal Mazarin's valet de chambre

Beringhen, Secretary to the Queen Mother

Bregy, musketeer

A Sergeant

Anne of Austria

Madame Henriette

Marie de Mancini

Miss de la Motte

Georgette

Charlotte

Gentlemen, Guards, Pages, Lackeys, Pikemen

The Action takes place at Vincennes 25-26 September 1658.

ACT I

The Council Hall in the Château Vincennes. Door at the back, door at the right—window on the left. A dozen morocco arm chairs and a large round table draped in green—the only furniture.

MAZARIN

(entering)

This way, my dear Mister Poquelin, this way.

POQUELIN

(following behind Mazarin, a notebook in hand)

Yes, Milord, yes. I am here—I am adding up the ladies of honor. The ladies of honor—2000 pounds.

MAZARIN

Keep going, keep going! It's the total that's waiting for you.

POQUELIN

Milord is too honest to cheat a poor upholsterer who hardly earns five percent—not to mention the speed with which I execute Milord's orders.

MAZARIN

Execute! Execute! You were forewarned more than a month ago, my good friend.

POQUELIN

Oh! Milord—happily, I still have on me the letter from Mr. Bernouin, your valet de chambre—here, Milord, here it is.

MAZARIN

No need, my dear Mister Poquelin.

POQUELIN

Excuse me, but I want to read this letter to Your Eminence to remind you of a little paragraph.

MAZARIN

Remind me of a paragraph—what do you mean?

POQUELIN

(reading)

"My dear Mr. Poquelin, His Majesty, having decided that he will spend the hunting season in his Château, at Vincennes, you are invited to go at once to the said Château with all your workers, so that this residence, which is completely unfurnished because it was used as a state prison, will be ready by the 25th of the present month of September.

MAZARIN

(interrupting him)

Well, I don't see the point of that paragraph, Mister Poquelin.

POQUELIN

Here it is precisely, Milord.

(resuming reading)

Work nights and make your men work nights—if need be. The King won't concern himself with the expense—by order of Cardinal Mazarin—signed Bernouin, valet de chamber to His Eminence—the 7th of September 1658.

MAZARIN

Well—what's the matter?

POQUELIN

(pointing to the phrase with his finger)

Damn!—Look Milord.

MAZARIN

What?

POQUELIN

"Work nights and make your men work nights—if need be. The King won't concern himself with the expense." That's very plain, Milord, it seems to me.

MAZARIN

(tracing his finger on the letter)

What's that?

POQUELIN

That:—the King—

MAZARIN

Very fair! It's not the Cardinal—and as it's the Cardinal who is the treasurer, its with the Cardinal that you are dealing, Mister. Let's see the total, Mister Poquelin, the total—! Or we'll never be done with it.

POQUELIN

(presenting his notebook)

It's very easy, Milord, there's the total.

MAZARIN

Pardon, I prefer to do the addition myself.

(looking on the table)

Well—why your council table! There's neither paper nor pens nor ink on your council table.

POQUELIN

I'm going to call, and ask for what Your Eminence wishes.

MAZARIN

NO, no! That will make us lose time! It is 9:30 and the council will convene at 10:00. I will find some old paper in my pocket.

(pulls out a paper)

There! Now lend me your pencil.

(he sits)

Oh! How it hurts on your armchairs, Mr. Poquelin—! Let's see—you say "Dining room—2,000 pounds."

(writing)

2,000 pounds. "Bedrooms for the King, the Queen, The Duke of Anjou, 4,000 pounds." Oh, Mr. Poquelin, if it weren't for the King—! But it is for the King.

(writing)

4,000 pounds. "Bedroom for Her Majesty, the Queen of England—and for Madam Henriette, her daughter—2,000 pounds." I ask you one little thing, they were so well off at the Louvre, what did they need to come to Vincennes for?

Anyway, since we must, let's add 2,000 pounds. "Bedroom for His Eminence, Cardinal Julio Mazarin, ante chamber for his petite lever and his grand lever—office for Mr. Bernouin, his valet de chambre—8,000 pounds—" as to that, there's nothing to say and it's not too expensive.

(writing)

8,000 pounds. "For the bedroom of the very highborn lady

Marie de Mancini, niece of His Eminence, the Cardinal—3,000 pounds." Three thousand pounds for the chamber of that little fir? Oh! Oh! Mr. Poquelin.

POQUELIN

Milord, I received, on that subject, a particular recommendation.

MAZARIN

And from whom, I beg you?

POQUELIN

From Mr. Bontemps, valet de chambre to His Majesty, who came to find me and who ordered me, on behalf of the King, to neglect nothing that was appropriate for the apartment of Miss Mancini.

MAZARIN

Ah! Ah!

POQUELIN

Yes, Milord.

MAZARIN

Bontemps—that fine Bontemps! On behalf of His Majesty!

POQUELIN

It's as I have the honor to tell you.

MAZARIN

(aside, rubbing his hands)

God! I had noticed indeed that the King was occupied with my niece.

(aloud)

Very well, Mr. Poquelin, very well! I'll overlook that, but it's over the rest we are going to have to squabble, I warn you. Hum! "Bedrooms for ladies of honor—2,000 pounds." Two thousand pounds, dear Mr. Poquelin—for people like that.

POQUELIN

There are six of them, Milord, it's 333 pounds per head.

MAZARIN

Eh! Death—we must make them double up—you are ruining us. Ah!

(writing)

Finally, for the Council Chamber, 1440 pounds. The Devil! Where are you going, Mr. Poquelin? Lucky for you, I'm in a hurry—we'll settle in round figures for 20,000 pounds.

POQUELIN

But consider, Milord—impossible!

MAZARIN

It's all agreed—you'll come get your payment order in a week.

POQUELIN

Milord, if this is an effect of your bounty.

MAZARIN

My bounty! My bounty! You know indeed that it is great. Look, my dear Poquelin, what do you ask of my bounty?

POQUELIN

Since Your Eminence has a pencil in your hand, it won't cost you any more to authorize this little sum right away—and in consideration of my getting the money in cash, I will agree to the reduction, Milord.

MAZARIN

And on what order? I'm in no condition to do it.

POQUELIN

Oh! I will content myself with this slip of paper. Milord's signature is excellent, and let Milord put there "good for 20,000 pounds," I wish he'd put "good for a million."

MAZARIN

Good for a million! And where do you want me to wind up? Why I'd have to sell myself down to my pins, dear Mr. Poquelin, to pay you a million—

(signing)

Here, since you absolutely will have it, but really, I have a weakness for you.

(he takes the scrap of paper and gives it to him)

POQUELIN

(opening the paper and reading)

Oh! Milord.

MAZARIN

Milord! Milord! What now?

POQUELIN

But Your Eminence has fixed payment for a year from now—look! 25 September 1659.

MAZARIN

Did I put one year?

POQUELIN

Yes indeed.

MAZARIN

I made a mistake, I thought I put two years. Give me back that paper, Mr. Poquelin—oh, this cursed fraud! This cursed fraud. It's ruined us completely.

POQUELIN

(clutching the paper)

Well, Milord, I will consent to wait—if Your Eminence will do me a favor—

MAZARIN

A favor? No!

POQUELIN

A favor which will cost Milord nothing.

MAZARIN

Then speak, go on!

POQUELIN

Milord knows I have the misfortune to have a son.

MAZARIN

Yes, that wise guy, Molière, who has made himself a poet and actor instead of accepting the inheritance of upholsterer to the King.

POQUELIN

Exactly, Milord—well if Milord would give me a letter de cachet to apprehend him and put him in prison until he renounces versifying and playacting.

MAZARIN

Well, my friend—

POQUELIN

Well, Milord, I think that I would willingly with satisfied to this note—although I haven't seen any money.

MAZARIN

Wow! Sign right away!

(starts to pass it to him, then stops)

No—indeed. The Devil.

POQUELIN

What, Milord?

MAZARIN

(aside)

I recalled this wise acre is protected by the Prince de Conti, my dear nephew, whose comrade and colleague he has been—Plague! His Highness would only get angry, seize the million I'd promised as a dowry for my niece, Anne Martinozzi. That would be to pay from my pocket and a bit too dearly, for furnishing the Château of Vincennes.

POQUELIN

Well, Milord?

MAZARIN

Well, my dear Poquelin, my desire to be agreeable to you was making me forget that letter de cachet, are affairs of state and consequently concern His Majesty—I don't meddle in affairs of state.

POQUELIN

What! Milord doesn't meddle in affairs of State?

MAZARIN

Oh! My dear friend! The King's reached his majority six years ago—address yourself to him.

POQUELIN

To the King? Why when could I see the King?

MAZARIN

Whenever you like. Tomorrow, today, in an hour—His Majesty must even already be here. There's a great hunting party in the forest, after the council, where we are meeting to try to come up with a little money—as upholsterer valet de chambre to the King—you have your entry everywhere—try to seize His Majesty and make him sign your invoice—pistol to the throat, Mr. Poquelin, stick him up!

POQUELIN

(aside)

Oh! If ever my rogue of a son writes a play about a miser, and has trouble finding a model, I will be able to furnish him one.

MAZARIN

You were saying, my dear Mr. Poquelin?

POQUELIN

I was saying I will see the King, Milord.

MAZARIN

Yes, affair of state—that concerns the King—Go! Mr. Poquelin, go!

(Poquelin, starting to leave meets Anne of Austria, the Queen Mother—at the door.)

POQUELIN

Ah! Her Majesty the Queen.

ANNE

Ah! It's you, Poquelin? I was looking for you.

POQUELIN

Your Majesty knows I am at her orders.

ANNE

So much the better, because I have a rush job for you.

POQUELIN

For me, Madame?

ANNE

For you—follow Beringhen and he will explain to you what I want.

POQUELIN

(bowing)

Majesty!

ANNE

Then, when the thing is finished, you will go to the King, Beringhen, and tell him that I'm expecting him.

BERINGHEN

Yes, Majesty. Come, Mr. Poquelin.

MAZARIN

Without too much curiosity, Madame, dare I ask you what Beringhen and Poquelin have to do together?

ANNE

They have to furnish an apartment, Cardinal. But don't worry, I am paying for the furnishing from my privy purse.

MAZARIN

One apartment?

ANNE

Yes—does that trouble you?

MAZARIN

The Queen knows I've had an apartment furnished for her, an

apartment for the King and one for the Duke of Anjou.

ANNE

Rooms, Cardinal.

MAZARIN

Rooms or an apartment—it's still the same thing—one for the Queen of England—one for her daughter, one for me and my niece, Marie—and six rooms for the ladies of honor.

ANNE

I've just visited them, sir.

MAZARIN

Well?

ANNE

Well, for all that, you see how demanding I am! I find them not enough apartments.

MAZARIN

The Queen is expecting someone?

ANNE

Exactly.

MAZARIN

It's a secret?

ANNE

Of the family, yes, Milord, but which may become a state secret.

MAZARIN

Well, I am a bit of the family—

ANNE

And much in the state! Under that double title, you indeed have the right to be in our confidence—that's quite true—are we alone?

MAZARIN

Quite alone—and except for the Musketeer who's promenading before the door—but—

ANNE

But, by speaking low, you mean, it's as if he wasn't and at Court one is used to speaking low.

(she signals Mazarin, who comes closer and leans on her armchair)

Cardinal?

MAZARIN

Madame?

ANNE

Have you considered sometimes that the King is of the age to be married?

MAZARIN

Damn! I think so, indeed. I not only thought that—and, here, just now, there in that armchair—I was thinking of it, and I said, like you.

(rubbing his hands)

"The King is of the age to get married."

ANNE

Ah, really!

(looking at Mazarin)

Do you have some idea for it?

MAZARIN

Me, Madame? No!

ANNE

More than once we've searched together for the wife that could suit him.

MAZARIN

It's true; we've passed in review all the marriageable princesses—and unfortunately for one reason or another, none could be Queen of France.

ANNE

The Infanta, Marie Therese suited us in every respect, and if she hadn't been an only child and consequently, destined to the throne of Spain—then at least until my sister-in-law the Queen of Spain, who is pregnant, puts a son into the world—we absolutely mustn't think of the Infanta.

MAZARIN

Alas, no!

ANNE

Still, the King is growing, sir, the King is becoming a man—the King is twenty. With the years, the passions of youth are going to succeed the caprices of childhood—up to now, he's only been amorous—but one day, a grave matter—he's going to love—a real passion may succeed all his caprices!

MAZARIN

Real! Ah! And for whom?

ANNE

How do I know—for some miss more clever and more ambitious than the others who, carefully directed by her relatives will cause him to do something stupid.

MAZARIN

Ah! Your Majesty fears that?

ANNE

Yes, and that's why I'm taking my precautions. Until now, the King has obeyed us, Cardinal—the King fears you and he loves me. We have kept, even over his youth, the power that our age had the right to claim over his childhood and against which, trust me—he's about ready to revolt. Let the struggle begin seriously—I know his character; he will curb us as well as the others, sir!

MAZARIN

Eh! Eh! Madame, I am constrained to confess there is much truth in what you just said.

ANNE

Oh—completely—sir—it's all true!

MAZARIN

Well, what has Your Majesty decided?

ANNE

A thing that I am going to tell you, Cardinal, and that I have yet to tell anyone. I have written to my sister-in-law, Christine de France, widow of Duke Amadeus of Savoy to come spend several days with us—and to bring Marguerite, her daughter, a charming child of seventeen, of whom I hope the King will become amorous—Marguerite will play a very agreeable role— don't you think, Cardinal?

MAZARIN

(pensive)

Indeed! I think so, Madame.

ANNE

That's why I need an apartment in addition to those already prepared—I am expecting tonight or tomorrow—the Duchess Christine and Princess Marguerite.

MAZARIN

Good.

ANNE

And by means of Beringhen, I warned the King to come join me here.

MAZARIN

Your Majesty intends to put him au courant of your projects?

ANNE

Not at all! That would put him on guard against what I desire. On the contrary, I intend that he see in his Cousin Marguerite only an ordinary visitor—Ah! Here's my messenger!

(Enter Beringhen.)

ANNE

Well, Beringhen?

BERINGHEN

Madame, the King has not yet arrived from Paris, or at least, no one has yet seen him at Vincennes.

ANNE

(meaningfully)

Ah, really? And Miss Mancini—has she arrived?

BERINGHEN

Yes, Madame, for I just noticed her at her window.

ANNE

And her window gives on the road to Paris, it seems to me? Right, Cardinal?

MAZARIN

I think so, yes.

ANNE

Why this troubles me, this absence of the King—look into it, Mazarin. You must know people who know better than we where he might be. Although you probably haven't thought of it, you want Louis to be present at the Council which is going to take place, right?

MAZARIN

Yes, Madame, yes—I certainly desire that he be there—Louis and all the gentlemen we have here.

ANNE

Go then, Mazarin, and look with your own eyes. You know the new fable of Fontaine—the Master's eye?

MAZARIN

I'm going there, Madame, I'm going there.

(aside)

Oh—she suspects something.

(leaving)

ANNE

(watching the Cardinal leave)

Beringhen.

BERINGHEN

Madame?

ANNE

You haven't told me all you had to tell me, right?

BERINGHEN

(eyes on the antechamber)

No, Madame, not all.

ANNE

At the moment of departure the King wasn't more particularly attentive to one person than another?

BERINGHEN

Indeed, Madame! He accompanied Miss Mancini, riding by her carriage door in hunt costume, and that as far as the Faubourg Saint Antoine; there only he took leave of her.

ANNE

Do you know what he said when he left her?

BERINGHEN

Here's what was heard; as Miss Mancini exhibited fear that this sitting of Parliament announced for today would delay the promised hunting party, "Miss," said the King, "You can assure those who question you on this subject that there are not a hundred lawyers assembled in the Palace of Justice who will prevent me from a shooting a stag at the agreed time." And with these words he turned back with Saint-Aignan, de Villeroi and de Guiche, and returned to Paris at a gallop.

ANNE

(pensive)

To Paris! Where could he have gone?

GUITAUT

(entering dressed in leather doublet and the military style of the end of Louis XIII's reign)

(abruptly)

If I am bothersome, I ask pardon to retire, Your Majesty.

ANNE

Bothersome, you, Guitaut? Never—on the contrary, I am always happy to see you and glad to speak to you.

(giving him her hand to kiss)

GUITAUT

Well, it's the same with me, Majesty—I am always happy when I see you—and satisfied when I speak to you.

ANNE

(to Beringhen)

Beringhen, take a walk in the courtyard without losing sight of the gate—and as soon as the King arrives let me know, if it is possible, where he's coming from and where he's going—

BERINGHEN

(leaving)

Yes, Madame.

ANNE

Come, Guitaut, come—you are my old friend.

GUITAUT

And I boast of it.

ANNE

You are right, for you've given me more than one proof of friendship.

GUITAUT

Your Majesty means devotion?

ANNE

I will never forget that it was you who led Louis XIII to the Louvre, on the evening of December 5, 1637.

GUITAUT

And who after leading him to the Louvre pushed him into your chamber where he hadn't been for six years and which he didn't leave until 9:00 of the next morning.

ANNE

(smiling behind her veil)

You have a fine memory, Guitaut.

GUITAUT

Good! And if memory weakens, King Louis XIV, born September 1638, will be a living memory to refresh it.

ANNE

But that's not all you did for me, Guitaut.

GUITAUT

No, in my character as Captain of the Guards, I had the advantage of arresting by your order first, the Duke of Beaufort, then Mr. de Condé, then Mr. de Conti, then Mr. de Longueville—let's not talk of Mr. de Conti nor Mr. de Longueville. Those I gave you cheaply enough but, without boasting of myself, many would not have thought my hand steady enough. But to take the King of the Halles and the Victor of Rocroy by the scruff of the neck.

ANNE

And then, my dear Guitaut, you also arrested Broussel.

GUITAUT

Bah! A councilor! That's not worth mentioning.

ANNE

Then Mr. de Gondy.

GUITAUT

No, Your Majesty is in error, it was Villequier who did his business.

ANNE

Ah! That's true! But what do you want, my dear Guitaut, we only loan to the rich.

GUITAUT

Gad! I wasn't there when the thing was done—I really regret it!
And if Your Majesty had deigned to write me, as King Henry
IV wrote to Crillon, "Hang yourself, Guitaut," I think word of a
gentleman—I'd have hung myself—

ANNE

Then, if the opportunity arose of giving me some new proof of
devotion of the same type—

GUITAUT

Let the Queen wink or gesture—like this or that and the one
who the Queen has had the honor to point out to me—is on the
way to the Bastille.

ANNE

Whoever it may be.

GUITAUT

Whoever it may be! I find it's been a long while since I arrested
anyone.

ANNE

Silence, my dear Guitaut! Someone's coming.

(The side door opens.)

GUITAUT

Oh—it's not someone it's the Duke of Anjou.

(aside, withdrawing and twirling his mustache)

Oh, oh—are the good times returning when they caress me like this?

(The Duke of Anjou enters.)

ANNE

It's you, Philippe.

D'ANJOU

Yes, Madame.

ANNE

Oh—luckily there's no one here and you can call me mother.

D'ANJOU

So much the better! For I have a favor to ask of you.

ANNE

What?

D'ANJOU

But, first of all—how do you find me this morning—little mommy?

ANNE

Much too handsome for a man

D'ANJOU

Good! You, too? Can you imagine the Chevalier de Lorraine fixed me up a pomade for my lips—here look at my lips—

ANNE

Indeed, they are adorably fresh.

D'ANJOU

And Guiche brought me a paste for the teeth—see?

ANNE

Your teeth are so beautiful, my child, they don't need paste.

D'ANJOU

There's nothing so handsome, little mommy, that cannot be embellished.

ANNE

But then why do you want to be so handsome, I ask you?

D'ANJOU

Why, to please, of course!

ANNE

Look at the King—does he spend his time at his toilette?

D'ANJOU

The King is the King—he has no need to please—since he can command.

ANNE

When you came, you spoke to me of a favor—

D'ANJOU

Oh, yes, it's true.

ANNE

Well?

D'ANJOU

Oh, it's a thing which I really want, I warn you, little mommy, ah, by the way, have you seen my Spanish leather gloves?

ANNE

No, but I see them.

D'ANJOU

It's Manicamp who made them for me—huh! How nice they smell! You who adore perfume—this must agree with you.

ANNE

Beware! If through strength of loving them, you are going to make me take them in hate.

D'ANJOU

Oh! There's no danger.

(imitating Mazarin's accent)

"With perfume and two beautiful strings, one could lure Queen Anne of Austria to hell."

ANNE

Well, sir!

D'ANJOU

It wasn't I, little mommy, who said that—it was the Cardinal!

ANNE

And your request? Let's see!

D'ANJOU

That's right! Here's what it is. It seems that Conti is a very wise prince, he was raised by the Jesuits of Clemont with the son of our upholsterer Poquelin.

ANNE

Yes, and what of it?

D'ANJOU

Ah—speaking of the upholsterer—how badly furnished it is here! And these cushions—are they hard! They're breaking my legs.

ANNE

(laughing)

You know that Mr. Mazarin is thrifty.

D'ANJOU

Oh, yes, and my brother also knows it. You remember the day the Superintendent of Finances gave Louis 200 crowns?

ANNE

Yes—

D'ANJOU

And when that poor brother had the impudence to make them clink in his breeches, Mr. de Mazarin said to him with his charming Eyetie accent, "What did I hear, my dear prince? You have some money, I believe" and took his 200 crowns, although Louis fought bravely for them.

ANNE

Hush! Let's not speak ill of Cardinal Mazarin, who loves you so much!

D'ANJOU

Him? He makes me brush my teeth, but in the end he cannot make me suffer—I am sure of it.

ANNE

Philippe!

D'ANJOU

You're right, little mommy. Let's return to my request. Well, this son of our upholsterer who's called Molière, it seems he's a deserving lad. Mr. de Conti offered him a situation as his secretary—which he refused. It's true that as Mr. de Conti is a little lively—they say he killed the last secretary with a pair of fire tongs, which is not engaging for the new one—you will agree—still this Molière is a fanatic for theater—he creates comedies which he plays himself—ah, when's there going to be a new ballet? The costume of the Nymph Echo looked so well on me.

ANNE

I think your brother would like nothing better than to dance a new one—but money is lacking.

D'ANJOU

What do you mean, money is lacking? I thought that the decrees were issued.

ANNE

Oh—but the Parliament is refusing to register them.

D'ANJOU

Oh! What a misfortune! The villainous Parliament! As for me, I always thought there was no good to be extracted from people so ugly and so badly dressed—! So to get back to the protégé of Mr. de Conti, the nephew of the Cardinal.

ANNE

Again—?

D'ANJOU

He wants—ah, my God—what's it called—? He wants—ah, I've got it—a privilege of a theater?

ANNE

Oh—but a privilege of a theater—that concerns the King.

D'ANJOU

The King?

ANNE

Yes, it's a great affair! An affair of State!

D'ANJOU

Then affairs of state—concern my brother?

ANNE

Doubtless, since he is king—

D'ANJOU

But war then—that's not an affair of state; Peace is not an affair of state, finances—that's not an affair of state—foreign alliances—that's not an affair of state.

ANNE

Why's that?

D'ANJOU

Hell, since you take care of them—you and Mazarin—little mommy—heavens! Do you want me to tell you—I'm afraid my poor brother Louis the XIV much resembles our august father, Louis XIII to whom Cardinal Richelieu, the great Cardinal as he's called now that he's dead—left to the royal office only the privilege of curing the scrofula.

ANNE

Will you shut up, wicked child?

D'ANJOU

Well, as for me, my little mommy, I am not such a great politician as Anne of Austria, or especially Cardinal Mazarin, but if I were in this place, well, word of honor, I would find something for that poor Louis to do for fear that one fine day.

ANNE

Well?

D'ANJOU

For fear that one fine day, as no one wants to place him in charge of anything, he'll put himself in charge of everything—war, peace, finances, alliances, marriage. Take it for sure—Meanwhile, as Molière is at my place—seeing that when he learned his father was at Vincennes, he had only one thing to fear—that of meeting his father, who they say wants to put him in the Bastille. Then, I say, as Molière's at my place, as the privilege of the theater reside, as they assure me in the great attributes reserved to the King, I am going to engineer Molière an interview with Louis, and my word! He will rub noses with the great prince as if he knew him. As for me, I will have done all I can do in this great affair.

(looking in the mirror of his mother's fan)—

Until I fix my wig.

ANNE

Silence!

D'ANJOU

(looking toward the door)

I should think so: Silence! Here come the great crown councilors—Cardinal at their head. Mr. Tellier, the Superintendent of Finances, I like him well enough—he's the one who keeps the money—he always is offering it—and sometimes he gives it—unluckily, the Parliament refuses what he offers and the Cardinal reclaims what he's giving! Then Mr. de Villeroi, Mr. de Grammont, Mr. de Montglat, Mr. de Villequier, the whole council. Oh, how royally one is going to get bored here. Mama— where is my brother? I thought being here one of the privileges reserved to him and that they didn't have the right to be bored without him.

(Mazarin, La Tellier, Lyonne, the Superintendent of Finances, the Duke de Grammont, the Duke de Villeroi, the Marquis de Montglat, the Duke de Villequier, Guitaut and other gentlemen enter.)

MAZARIN

(who enters first)

Take seats, gentlemen.

(going to Anne of Austria)

Madame, no one knows where the King is, and on honor, I know no more than the others.

ANNE

Then proceed, Cardinal, proceed.

MAZARIN

Gentlemen, you know the reason you are assembled here. Under the presentation of the Superintendent of Finances, the decrees were signed by His Majesty; it contains loads of new things that render indispensable the needs of the state. Day before yesterday, Parliament, intimidated doubtless by the presence of the King, promised to en-register the decrees—but yesterday and today, Parliament has reneged, or so it seems, on its promise—there's a large assembly of these gentlemen at the palace of justice. In your opinion, gentlemen, what must be done ?

GUITAUT

We must arrest the Parliament and stuff them into the Bastille.

MAZARIN

Who said that?

GUITAUT

(advancing)

I did, b'god!

MAZARIN

Ah! It's you, my dear Guitaut? Hello, Guitaut!

GUITAUT

Put me in charge of the operation and it will be soon done.

MAZARIN

Gentlemen, you've heard Mr. Guitaut's proposal—what do you say about it?

LE TELLIER

The Parliament is a body with whom one must reckon, they've taught us that, Milord.

LYONNE

It has a right of remonstrance.

SUPERINTENDENT

Yes, but it doesn't have a right of refusal.

DUKE de GRAMMONT

Gentlemen, here's what I propose.

MAZARIN

Hear the Duke de Grammont, gentlemen, he's a man of wit.

DUKE de GRAMMONT

I thank Your Eminence, the compliment much, much more flattering than it was intended to be—

(Commotion in the antechamber.)

MAZARIN

Silence!

DUKE de GRAMMONT

Here's what I propose—

(the commotion increases)

BERINGHEN

(entering abruptly)

The King, gentlemen.

EVERYBODY

The King!

(The door opens: the King appears in red hunting gear—felt hat on his head, large hunting boots, whip in hand. Behind him, the youthful court, opposing through its costume the older one: Saint-Aignan, the Marquis de Villeroi, the Count de Guiche, etc., etc.,)

KING

Greetings, gentlemen. There's a council meeting so it seems—?

MAZARIN

Sire, Your Majesty finds us occupied deliberating over this meeting of the Parliament and to find a way of getting these gentlemen to en-register the edicts.

KING

Unnecessary, gentlemen, the edicts have been en-registered.

ALL

En-registered?

MAZARIN

And who brought about this miracle, Sire?

KING

I did, Cardinal.

MAZARIN

But how was Your Majesty able to attain—?

KING

I've been to the Parliament myself.

MAZARIN

And Your Majesty made a speech?

KING

I said 'I wish it'!

(Mazarin and the Queen exchange a glance.)

D'ANJOU

Bravo, Louis—

KING

And now, gentlemen—

(looking at his watch)

it is eleven o'clock; I set the departure for the hunt at noon time. So change into hunt costumes—for the departure will sound at noon exactly. My Mother—Cardinal—I hope indeed you will do us the honor of being part of our hunt.

ANNE

Yes, my son.

(she leaves first.)

MAZARIN

Yes, Sire.

(he leaves next)

D'ANJOU

Stay a few seconds in this room, Louis: I have a protégé who's going to come ask you a favor.

KING

And you, go get dressed, and try not to be long if it's possible.

D'ANJOU

Oh, I cannot answer for anything! Anyway, if I am not ready, I'll join you.

(leaves)

DUKE de GRAMMONT

(aside to councilors)

Well, gentleman, what do you say to what's just happened ?

DUKE de VILLEROI

It seems to me my pupil works miracles!

MONTGLAT

The King appears to me to have decided to be King—absolutely.

GUITAUT

As for me, I say he won't really be King until he's ordered me to arrest someone and he hasn't—yet!

(general exit)

KING

(alone)

She was at her window! Who was she expecting if not me?
God knows! Perhaps Saint-Aignan, perhaps Villeroi, perhaps
Guiche—it seems to me—still, that it really was me she
greeted—Bah!—one always greets the King—whoever he may
be. Oh! If I were sure that she truly loved me, that would give
me courage! Strange thing—this fear I cannot overcome. I, who
raised the whip to this Parliament as on a pack of hound dogs—

(he makes a gesture of striking—the whip escapes his hands
and rolls under the table)

I tremble before a young girl! It's true I still tremble a bit before
my mother and a lot before the Cardinal!

(gets down on his knees to get the whip. When he pulls up the
table covering, he notices a young girl very coquettishly dressed
as a peasant)

What's this? Who is there? What are you doing, child?

GEORGETTE

Oh, excuse me, Sire! Sire—pardon!

KING

Why, I'm not mistaken—no, yes, yes! It's you child?

GEORGETTE

Oh—the King remembers me? How lucky!

KING

Yes—you are the daughter of Papa Dupre.

GEORGETTE

Yes, Sire.

KING

Who was the junior gardener at Castle Saint German?

GEORGETTE

He's just been named Gardener in Charge of the Château de Vincennes.

KING

We played together a hundred times in the flower beds of the New Castle—and the fortifications of Old Castle—your name is—wait a second—your name is Georgette.

GEORGETTE

Yes, Georgette the Curious—because they always found me hidden somewhere, behind some curtain or under some table— looking and listening—that's it.

KING

(laughing)

Well, it seems you've grown and improved, but you haven't changed your name, eh?

GEORGETTE

The King believes I was here from curiosity?

KING

Hell, it looks that way to me—

GEORGETTE

Oh—the King is much mistaken.

KING

Why were you there then—hmm?

GEORGETTE

Because I was scared.

KING

Afraid of whom?

GEORGETTE

Of His Eminence, the Cardinal.

KING

And for what reason?

GEORGETTE

Because—because—I am not bold enough to tell Your Majesty.

KING

Miss Georgette.

GEORGETTE

Sire—

KING

Take care! I am going to say "I wish it!"

GEORGETTE

Like at Parliament!

KING

(to himself)

Charming—this little girl!

GEORGETTE

The King is very good.

KING

What—you heard?

GEORGETTE

Oh—I've a clever ear.

KING

Come, tell me this, child—why were you hidden under this table?

GEORGETTE

The King won't get mad?

KING

No—anyway, it's not the King you're telling, it's your playmate, Louis.

GEORGETTE

The King still remembers—?

KING

If you have a clever ear, Georgette, as for me, I've got a good memory.

GEORGETTE

Then—that reassures me—!

KING

I'm listening.

GEORGETTE

Well, Sire—I must tell you what's been done—for the last week, a great hullabaloo at Château Vincennes.

KING

I suspect so.

GEORGETTE

Everybody going and coming, shouting, "They say the King's going to come. Mr. Poquelin has come to furnish the Château— He's going to have hunts, balls, parties."

KING

And you? And what did you say when you learned that?

GEORGETTE

As for me, I clapped my hands and I said, "So much the better! So much the better."

KING

And why did you say so much the better?

GEORGETTE

That's exactly what my father asked me.

KING

Any you answered him—?

GEORGETTE

I answered him—"So much the better, because the King is one of my good friends and we will play together again in the gardens and in the apartments like before!"

KING

Why do you know you are adorable, Georgette?

GEORGETTE

Me? Oh! How funny for you to say that to me, Sire.

KING

(taking her hand)

And you answered your father—? Say, look here, what a pretty little hand.

GEORGETTE

No, it was my father who replied in his turn, he said, "Hush Georgette! You mustn't say things like that. The King is no longer a little boy exiled from Paris by the Fronde—who played with you in the gardens of Saint Germain—he's a handsome young man—he's a great prince—and there's even a poet, Mr. de Benserade, who says he's a god—

KING

Really? A poor god, on my word, Georgette—a god without Olympus and without thunder.

GEORGETTE

Then, I felt myself becoming more curious than ever. I'd seen young handsome men—but I'd never seen a god—except in marble and in the gardens of the New Château—"Oh," I said to myself, "I want to see a god in the flesh and bone, the first in all the world." Then this morning, knowing that you were going to arrive from Paris, I slipped into this big room, and I put myself in this window which gives on the highway. I'd already seen many mortals enter, but not one god, when suddenly I heard a noise behind me. I turned around, it was Cardinal Mazarin who was coming with the Upholsterer—you remember, Sire, before we used to be very frightened of Cardinal Mazarin—both of us?

KING

Even now, I'm in great fear of him.

GEORGETTE

Ah! Look, that proves that in my place you would have done like me.

KING

What did you do?

GEORGETTE

Can't you guess? I dove under the table. Gosh, I thought his accounts with the upholsterer finished they'd go away—both of them. Not at all, the upholsterer left—enter the Queen Mother—of whom we were both once so afraid—also—you remember, Sire?

KING

Yes—I'm still afraid, but a bit less now.

GEORGETTE

Then they began to speak of affairs of state—

KING

That must have amused you!

GEORGETTE

Oh, Sire, it bored me terribly! Still, since it was question of your marriage—oh—then I listened, I listened.

KING

What do you mean of my marriage?

GEORGETTE

Yes, it seems you are going to marry—but hush! You're not supposed to know.

KING

What do you mean, not supposed to know?

GEORGETTE

No—it's a big secret! Only the Queen Mother and Cardinal Mazarin in the whole world know about this project. And yet, this morning the Cardinal didn't know it, it's the Queen Mother who had got there ahead of his foresight. That's almost the way she expressed it and who confided it to him.

KING

So—they want to marry me without my knowing it?

GEORGETTE

I think that is their intention.

KING

But still—who do they intend to marry me to?

GEORGETTE

Oh, Gosh, I don't know if I can tell you.

KING

What do you mean, you don't know if you can tell me? You not only can—you must!

GEORGETTE

Are you sure?

KING

Yes, under penalty of rebellion to your King—! Are you a rebel, Georgette?

GEORGETTE

No, Sire!

KING

Well then speak up! Who are they going to marry me to?

GEORGETTE

With Princess Marguerite of Savoy.

KING

With my cousin?

GEORGETTE

Ah—she's your cousin, Sire?

KING

All princesses are my cousins, Georgette. Ah! So it's with Marguerite of Savoy they're going to marry me?

GEORGETTE

Yes, and she's arriving today or tomorrow with her Mama Christine—only you understand, Sire, they are coming to visit Her Majesty, the Queen, not for anything else.

KING

Yes.

GEORGETTE

And as the Princess is very pretty, very witty, very charming— they hope she will combat your love.

KING

(excitedly)

My love for whom?

GEORGETTE

Ah—I don't know. Your love for the person you may love.

KING

Ah! Ah! It's good to know what you just told me, Georgette. And is that all you heard?

GEORGETTE

All! Isn't that enough, Sire?

KING

Oh, yes, yes! What a good thing you did by hiding yourself.

GEORGETTE

Really? How happy I am! Then I will always hide myself.

KING

And you will come tell me all you hear?

GEORGETTE

All!

KING

Then they didn't say anything else?

GEORGETTE

Relative to the King? No, Mr. Poquelin asked for a letter de cachet against his son, but the Cardinal answered 'That concerns the King.' Affairs of State! The Duke d'Anjou asked the Queen mother for a theater license for Mr. Molière—but the Queen replied 'That's King's business. Affair of State.' So in the matter, it's agreed Mr. Poquelin will come himself to ask you for the letter de cachet against his son—and that Mr. Molière will solicit in person the theater license. That's what the Duke d'Anjou begged you to remain in this room for.

KING

And there's nothing more?

GEORGETTE

No, sire, this time there's nothing more. I am quite sure of it.

KING

What a pretty police officer I've got here—

(looking around him)

GEORGETTE

The King desires something?

KING

Yes, Miss Georgette the Curious! I want to know who is the Musketeer on guard.

(calling)

Mr. Musketeer!

BOUCHAVANNES

(stopping in the doorway)

The King called?

KING

Yes, sir—I want you to take a description of this child here, and give it to your comrades so she may pass freely to see me whenever she wishes—anyway, her name will be her passport—she's called Georgette.

BOUCHAVANNES

The King will be obeyed.

GEORGETTE

Oh—how happy I am!

KING

Just a moment, sir.

BOUCHAVANNES

Sire?

KING

Aren't you Mr. de Bouchavannes?

BOUCHAVANNES

Yes, Sire.

KING

Then you've arrived from Turin? It seems to me they had me sign a leave for you.

BOUCHAVANNES

I came from Turin a week ago, Sire—and I spent three months there, my mother having the honor to be a lady of the Regent's Palace.

KING

Come here, if you please, sir.

(Bouchavannes leaves his pike on the doorway and comes forward.)

BOUCHAVANNES

Sire.

KING

You must know the Princess Marguerite?

BOUCHAVANNES

I had the honor to see her, almost every day and to speak to her two or three times.

KING

And what kind of person is she?

BOUCHAVANNES

The King does me the honor to question me about her physically or morally?

KING

On both counts, sir.

GEORGETTE

(picking up the pike and barring the door to Poquelin)

No one can come in!

KING

That's it, Georgette. Stand good guard in the place of Mr. Bouchavannes.

POQUELIN

Sire!

KING

Ah, it's you, Mr. Poquelin? Right in a moment.

POQUELIN

(withdrawing)

Sire!

GEORGETTE

(replacing the pike)

There!

KING

Let's go back to our interrogation, sir.

BOUCHAVANNES

Well, Sire, the Princess Marguerite is morally a pious and charitable Princess, worthy in every respect of the blood she comes
from.

KING

And physically? I want an exact portrait, Mr. de Bouchavannes.

BOUCHAVANNES

Sire—black hair, big melancholy eyes, a complexion more calm
than animated—a well formed nose, fresh lips, white teeth,
graceful and flexible figure. Anyway, if the King wants more
precise information—

KING

Well?

BOUCHAVANNES

(smiling)

I have the advantage of knowing a young girl attached to the princess in the capacity of maid of honor—

KING

Thanks, Mr. de Bouchavannes, I know all that I want to know. If you are not on duty this evening—which is likely, since you are on duty this morning—

BOUCHAVANNES

Pardon, Sire! We are few in number—24 in all.

KING

I know the Cardinal practices monetary economies but I was unaware he was economical with the Musketeers.

BOUCHAVANNES

So much so that we have two shifts every 24 hours—my second comes tonight, from nine to eleven in the Orangery.

KING

Well, before nine, come while the gaming is going on, come by chance. I will be pleased to see you there and perhaps need to ask you more information. You are a good gentleman, as I understand it, sir.

BOUCHAVANNES

Sire, my father had the honor of riding in the carriage of King Louis XIII.

KING

That's fine—we'll try to find you a company, sir.

BOUCHAVANNES

Oh, Sire!

(giving a military salute and resuming his station)

KING

And now let Mr. Poquelin enter.

POQUELIN

(entering)

Sire!

KING

(making a sign with his hand)

Georgette, leave me with this brave gentleman—you have no need to hear what he's going to tell me—you already know.

GEORGETTE

Yes.

KING

While elsewhere perhaps you will learn something you don't know.

GEORGETTE

I'll try.

KING

Go—you have free access to me at all times.

GEORGETTE

Thanks, Sire! I will profit by it.

(aside)

Oh—he doesn't resemble all those marble gods at all.

(she leaves)

KING

Approach, Mr. Poquelin!

POQUELIN

(trembling and fumbling with a bunch of papers which he drops and picks up)

KING

I know what it is—a petition right? Give it to me.

POQUELIN

Yes, Sire, a petition.

KING

Begging to have your son, Molière, locked up because he dishonors the name of Poquelin.

POQUELIN

What! The King knows—?

KING

Yes, I know a lot of things that no one suspects I know—so that Molière?

POQUELIN

Oh, Sire! The wretch! He's brought shame to our family. A poet and an actor!

KING

Still, it seems to me that a poet—

POQUELIN

A poet—may be okay—although when he had before him a situation as sure and honorable as that of upholsterer—it seems to me a great folly, to risk dying of starvation by embracing poetry—but, still, at least there are gentlemen who meddle with it—Where as an actor, Sire—! A man who puts powder on his face, oh!

KING

Well, don't worry, I'll look into it—

POQUELIN

Then I may hope ?

KING

That justice will be given to whoever is right. Go, Mr. Poquelin, go.

POQUELIN

Ah, Sire, you are saving the honor of a family.

(he leaves)

KING

(alone, sitting down)

What strange places pride is to be found.

(opening the petition)

"Petition to obtain a letter de cachet against Jean-Baptiste Poquelin, who calls himself Molière—Sire—"

(noticing a paper)

Heavens, what's this—papers that slipped into Master Poquelin's petition—it's the Cardinal's handwriting.

(reading)

"Dining room, 2,000 pounds—King's bedroom, Queen's 4,000 pounds—total, 20,000 pounds payable September 25, 1659. Mazarin."

Ah, this is the payment order that poor devil in his concern and indignation let slip in between the pages of his petition. I must return it to him.

(stopping)

Oh! Oh! What's this on the other side—Plague!—a round enough sum. "39 million 216 thousand pounds!" What's this? "State of the fortune of Cardinal Mazarin on 24 September 1658". Oh, my word—it was yesterday he couldn't find any more money.

(reading)

"On Lyon—3 million, 900 thousand pounds—"

"On Bordeaux 7 millions—"

"On Madrid 4 millions—"

"General income 7 million—"

"Value of lands, castles, palaces, houses woods, 9 million—"

"cash and diverse items of values, 2 million 600 thousand pounds—"

Ah, Mr. Mazarin—you who always cry poverty! Ah, but how did this precious paper get into the hands of Mr. Poquelin?

Ah, I understand—without paying attention to what was written on one side, Mazarin wrote on the other.

That's that, on my word. This is precious information and which ties in with the news Georgette announced to me. Good—someone's coming—it's doubtless that rascally son—

MOLIÈRE

(half opening the door from the Duke d'Anjou, timidly but not clumsily)

The King will excuse my badness, I hope—but Milord, the Duke of Anjou told me that His Majesty was forewarned of my visit.

KING

Come in, Mr. Molière! Come in! Yes, I am forewarned and I was expecting you.

MOLIÈRE

My God, Sire, the fear I have of hastening too much—has it made me fall into the opposite causing the King to be bored waiting for me?

KING

Yes, I was waiting for you, but rest assured, I didn't lose my time doing so.

MOLIÈRE

Sire, I will try to lay out my request in few words—but if I tire the King—at a sign from His Majesty, I will retire.

KING

Not at all, Mr. Molière! I am a man of first impression s—and my first impression of you—is that I like you.

MOLIÈRE

Sire!

KING

They torment you in your family. They persecute you, they make you very miserable, right?

MOLIÈRE

Sire, it's impossible for me to wish ill to my good parents. They are quite sincerely convinced that one who follows the career I have embraced will lose his body in this world and his soul in the next.

KING

And as for you—that's not your opinion—

MOLIÈRE

As for me, Sire, my opinion is that in every condition one can live like an honest man and that God is too just to damn honest men.

KING

Mr. de Conti was your school fellow.

MOLIÈRE

Yes, Sire—we studied together at the Jesuit College of Clermont.

KING

He is younger than you though.

MOLIÈRE

Oh, yes, Sire, much, much younger—for it was only late—that is to say at the age of 18, I obtained my father's permission to study.

KING

You studied law?

MOLIÈRE

I've even been received as an attorney, Sire, but it's not my vocation.

KING

You know that Mr. de Conti makes a great case for you—he pretends that if he were King—he would consult you on all matters of politics. He says you know rhetoric, philosophy, poetry—

MOLIÈRE

Sire, Mr. de Conti is too indulgent! It's true I studied rhetoric with Father Thuillier—and philosophy with Gassendi, but as for poetry—

KING

As for poetry? Finish, sir—

MOLIÈRE

Well, Sire, I think one cannot learn poetry—that one who is not born a poet will never become one.

KING

Ah, really? And tell me, Molière, let's see—what is a poet?

MOLIÈRE

Why, Sire, don't you have at court, by Your Majesty side, under your eyes folks who call themselves so?

KING

Who?

MOLIÈRE

Why Mr. de Benserade, for example, Mr. de Saint-Aignan, Sire.

KING

Would you like me to tell you something, Mr. Molière. Well, I have the notion that they are not true poets.

MOLIÈRE

Really, Sire?

KING

Yes.

(looking fixedly at him)

While as for you, you are one. Here's what I ask you—what's a poet?

MOLIÈRE

Sire, you've read before in Virgil the fable of Aristée the Shepherd?

KING

Yes, Mr. Molière.

MOLIÈRE

Well, in that fable, Sire, there's a certain Proteus, lion, serpent, flame, smoke, cloud, either forever escaping the chain which holds him—from the hand which tries to grasp him, from the eye which tries to analyze him. Sire, he's the poet. How can you expect me to explain such a character?

KING

Never mind! Try anyway. What you tell me is so different from the language in use in the country I live in that I feel as if I'm listening to a man speak for the first time.

MOLIÈRE

(what profound sadness)

The poet, Sire, is a man born hanging on a smile or a frown of nature—he's a composite of tears and joy—laughing like a child, weeping like a woman, forever letting reality escape him in the pursuit of a dream, valuing all the wealth of the earth no more than the cloud which slides across the sky and which changes twenty times a minute! It's the Roman Emperor desirous of the impossible, and who satisfied by the illusion takes a drop of water for a pearl, the glowworm for a star, caprice for love! It's rather the poor cricket singing in the grass, intoxicated by the odor of freshly cut hay—king of a world of cornflowers and daisies which he prefers even to your realm, Sire! He's rather the proud eagle soaring above the clouds, emperor of infinity, streaming in the gold of the sun, and altering from moment to moment, a raucous and savage scream which is only an expression of his powerlessness to mount higher and his sadness at being forced to descend. He's finally, the man that you could make as Mr. de Conti said, a councilor, secretary of state, prime minister that you could heap with all the favors of fortune and all the gifts of power—and who, when he has the honor of seeing his king, of speaking to him, of falling at his feet, asks of all gifts, solicits of all favors four boards, placed on four columns, shut in by four walls, on which he can cause to enter, leave, speak, act, declaim, laugh, weep and suffer—characters of fantasy who, locked in his imagination have existed only for him and who, nonetheless are his true family, his only world, his unique friends! That's the poet, Sire! And now there remains nothing left for me but to be astonished that such a strange creature has dared to present himself before the greatest, most noble, most powerful King in the universe—before King Louis XIV!

KING

Ah, my word! Mr. Molière, you have given me such a find definition of the poet that I will ask you one of king. That will be more difficult right?

MOLIÈRE

No, Sire.

KING

Well, Mr. Molière, what is a King?

MOLIÈRE

Sire, he's a man posterity curses when he's called Nero, and that future ages bless when he's called Henry IV.

KING

And, in your opinion, Mr. Molière, if a King had to ask God to grant him a gift, what gift ought he to demand?

MOLIÈRE

Solomon asked for wisdom.

KING

But as for me, I don't wish to do what was done before me, even by King Solomon.

MOLIÈRE

Well, Sire, the knowledge most precious for a King would be truth.

KING

Yes, but the way to know the truth?

MOLIÈRE

Eh! Sire, sometimes, it's by seeming to know it.

KING

Make me grasp what you are telling me.

MOLIÈRE

Alas, Sire, I am only a poor comic poet and cannot consequently, offer you any means but through comedy.

KING

Offer, Molière, it will be received.

MOLIÈRE

Well, Sire, suppose for example that chance had made you master of a secret.

KING

Chance has done better, Mr. Molière, for this very day, it delivered two to me—and of the greatest importance.

MOLIÈRE

Then chance is treating you like a spoiled child—and that proves its intelligence. Well, the King has done me the honor of remaining alone for a quarter of an hour with me.

KING

Yes.

MOLIÈRE

No one has seen me enter, no one will see me leave. Well, Sire, let the King say that his quarter of an hour was spent with a secret agent who delivers him an account of everything that's being said, even being thought at court. Let him slip the knowledge of these two secrets that he has in the ear of two persons who think these secrets are known to themselves alone. Let these persons tell what's just happened to them to a friend or confidant—and—I know men of the court—each one will come to tell you the secret of his neighbor—and perhaps even his own—for fear your secret agent has come to tell it to you before him.

KING

Oh—by heavens, Mr. Molière, what a jolly idea—and I adopt it.

MOLIÈRE

Sire, it's too much honor for the poor poet who gives it to you.

(the horn shrieks)

But.

(the departure sounds)

KING

It's the departure sounding, Now, listen, Mr. Molière, it's required that above all the poet who always takes reality for the shadow, have, at the final reckoning, something to eat—so from today, you are my honorary valet de chambre—with a salary of 3,000 pounds.

MOLIÈRE

Oh—sire, what kindness! And my license?

KING

You are my valet de chambre, Mr. Molière—you'll ask me whenever you like.

MOLIÈRE

Oh! Sire! to kiss the royal hand is now the only desire remaining to me.

(The King offers his hand. Molière kisses it respectfully and leaves—meanwhile, the antechamber fills with gentlemen in hunting costume.)

KING

Come gentlemen, to the hunt—and I hope that the day will end as well as it has begun.

(The King leaves and everyone follows him.)

CURTAIN

ACT II

The Forest of Vincennes—to the left, the oak of Saint Louis—to the right of a clump of trees and behind these trees a green grotto.

The King, Queen Anne, and the courtiers, male and female, with attendants, are present at rise, divided into groups— some seated, some standing, some lying down—the first group is under the oak of St. Louis—consisting of Anne, Madame Henriette, Miss de la Motte, de Beringhen, and the Chevalier de Lorraine—the second group to the right consists of the King, the Duke d'Anjou, Marie de Mancini, the Count de Guiche, the Marquis de Villeroi, and the Count de Dangeau. The third group is composed of the Cardinal, and the Dukes de Villeroi, de Grammont and Mr. de Villequier—rugs are on the ground, glasses and bottles strewn about. Hampers of food. It's the end of the picnic.

MARIE

(in a low voice, by a motion of her head indicating Dangeau, who's writing in his notebook)

Sire, ask Dangeau what he's doing. As for me, I bet, it's a madrigal in honor of your passion for Miss de la Motte who's looking at us with a ferocious eye, knowing that Her Majesty, the Queen Mother, cannot hear our words—or lose one of our gestures.

KING

First of all, you know better than anyone that Miss de la Motte has been, but no longer is, my passion. If I as yet don't have all the power of a King. I have the heart of one: Miss de la Motte having loved or still loving Mr. de Charmante, can no longer be anything for me. It follows, I know better than anyone, I to whom a secret agent has revealed everything that Dangeau doesn't write verse. So it's then impossible for two big lies to escape the so small and so charming mouth of Miss Marie de Mancini at the same time.

MARIE

Oh, Sire, that's the most gallant denial ever given me, even in the alcoves of Madame de Rambouillet.

D'ANJOU

Guiche, are you amused to hear love talked of ceaselessly?

GUICHE

To talk of it, yes, to hear it talked of—no—

MARIE

But finally, I am getting back to the bottom of things, as the beautiful Artenice says. How do you expect me to know, Sire, if Miss de la Motte is or is not your passion and whether Mr. Dangeau is or is not composing a madrigal?

KING

Because woman is not mistaken about the feeling she inspires, and her gaze penetrates as easily as love to the depth of the heart of her lover, as the diver seeing a pearl in the depths of the sea.

MARIE

Ah, Sire, why you are a poet! And if you try, I am sure of it, you will write verse as heartfelt as the Count de Saint-Aignan or the Marquis de la Feuillade.

D'ANJOU

Is that your opinion, Guiche?

GUICHE

Damn! Isn't the King the King? And in that capacity can't the King do whatever he pleases—? Anyway, poetry is feminine! Why like all women won't it be unfaithful or coquettish?

KING

Guiche, I warn you, if you continue to speak ill of women, I will exile you.

GUICHE

Like Charmante, Sire? Egad, that wouldn't surprise me.

D'ANJOU

As for me, I don't see myself much in verse. I love it a little more than sweetmeats a little less than lace, jewels and diamonds— for which I would sell my right of seniority if I were Essau instead of being Jacob—but I found the last quatrain by Mr. de la Feuillade badly rhymed—listen up—

MARIE

Oh! Milord, by chance did your governor make you learn the verse of Mr. de la Feuillade for a pension?

D'ANJOU

First of all, Miss Marie—know that for two years I haven't had a governor and that consequently, I alone govern myself. No, thank, God! I no longer have a governor and only perform those agencies imposed by Cardinal Mazarin—when his avarice refuses me money to buy lace. By the way—niece of your uncle, you've got some really marvelous English lace there.

MARIE

Her Majesty, Queen Henriette gave it to me.

D'ANJOU

Poor Aunt! Does she still have something to give? I thought Cromwell, father and son, had taken everything.

GUICHE

Get out, really! Now we're going to turn to politics.

D'ANJOU

Ah, indeed! Why you're never satisfied are you, Guiche?

MARIE

No, but Mr. de Guiche wants to remind Milord that my English lace made him forget Mr. de la Feuillade's verse.

D'ANJOU

Ah—well, here. He needs to rhyme luck with kiss—and Molière to whom I showed it, assures me it doesn't—sufficiently.

DUKE de VILLEROI

La Feuillade is a gentleman, Milord, and in that capacity, it seems to me he isn't obliged to rhyme like a peasant.

MARIE

But, in short, all this, Sire, doesn't tell us if Dangeau is writing verse or prose.

KING

We're going to learn. Come here, Dangeau!

DANGEAU

Here I am, Sire.

KING

Miss Mancini pretends you are writing verse. I pretend you are writing prose.

D'ANJOU

I bet—neither the one nor the other.

KING

Which of the two of us is right?

DANGEAU

You, as always, Sire.

KING

Take care, Dangeau! There are certain persons who must always be right against me—even when they are wrong.

DANGEAU

Sire, my character as a historian forbids me from ever lying.

D'ANJOU

And especially all flattery!

DANGEAU

I am forced to say it was history I am writing and one doesn't write history in verse.

KING

Well, let's see—read us your history.

DANGEAU

Sire, will you allow me to complete my sentence?

KING

Yes, finish it, finish it—

MISS DE LA MOTTE

Look, Madame—he's not taking his eyes of her for a moment.

ANNE

Alas, child, two weeks ago at the Louvre, Madame de Chatillon said the same thing about you.

MISS DE LA MOTTE

Oh, excuse me, Madame, but you cannot think.

ANNE

I can think—because I am three times your age, aren't I, child? But you know that women are always twenty in some spot in their heart.

KING

Have you finished, Dangeau?

DANGEAU

Yes, Sire.

KING

Then—we're listening to you.

DANGEAU

(reading with the greatest seriousness)

"The 25th of December 1658, His Majesty Louis XIV, before
the hunt, took his lunch in the Forest of Vincennes in the place
called the Oak of Saint Louis—the hunters ate on the turf,
divided into several groups. The group with the King was
composed of—

KING

(interrupting him)

Fine, fine, Dangeau. You've told us enough and we are convinced
now that it's not poetry you are composing.

D'ANJOU

Plague! What an interesting book you're composing, Dangeau—
if your history of the reign of my brother contains many para-
graphs like the one just read us!

ANNE

(calling)

Grammont.

GRAMMONT

(leaving Mazarin's group and going to the Queen)

Madame.

ANNE

What nasty story did you just tell the Cardinal that made you both laugh, you red, he green while that others didn't laugh at all.

GRAMMONT

Oh, Majesty! A simple joke! His Eminence neither eats nor drinks under the pretext that the poisoner of Guenaud had put him on a diet.

ANNE

And you find that funny?

GRAMMONT

That after having taken the ministry from Mr. de Beaufort, the Regency from Anne of Austria, liberty from Mr. de Condé, the Cardinalate from Pope Urbain, the Archepiscopacy of Paris from Mr. de Rety, royalty from the King, money from France, Cardinal de Mazarin cannot take a good stomach from a lackey in his antechamber or a poster on the street corner.

GUICHE

(rising and passing his hand over his face)

Ah!

(he moves off)

KING

What's the matter with Guiche? Just now he was growling and

now it seems he's sighing.

MARIE

How would I know?

KING

Good! You don't want to tell me. Let's not speak of it any more.
I will ask my secret agent about it.

MARIE

Pardon Sire, but this is the second time Your Majesty has spoken
of a secret agent—may one know what you employ this mysterious confidant for?

KING

To find out all that's said, done or thought at court. So, for
example, I have only to ask him what's going on in your heart—
he will tell me; what my cousin Henriette, who hasn't yet spoken
a single word and seems to me more ready to cry than laugh, is
thinking—and what Cardinal Mazarin is whispering so low to
the Duke de Villeroi—so the priestly skull cap of the one and
the hat of the other are not in on the secret of their words—well,
he will tell me.

MARIE

Oh—clever joke!

D'ANJOU

Dangeau, here's a thing to put in your memoirs. My brother
Louis has like that frightful Socrates, whose bust frightened

me so much while I was a child that I've taken a hatred to all philosophies past, present and future—my brother, Louis, has a familiar demon who haunts him by day and visits him by night.

ANNE

(who has listened with a certain attention)

What are you saying there, Philippe?

D'ANJOU

Madame, I'm playing, as already happened to me in the ballet the Four Seasons, the role of the Nymph, Echo. My brother Louis pretends to have a secret agent who repeats to him everything that is said, everything that is thought at court—so in the future there will be no longer any way to hide anything from him.

HENRIETTE

(trembling)

Oh! My God!

D'ANJOU

Well, does that frighten you, Henriette? Do you by chance have something to hide?

(to Miss de la Motte who signals him)

Huh?

HENRIETTE

(as d'Anjou talks with Miss de la Motte and Beringhen goes to get orders from Mazarin)

Madame, if that's true, what d'Anjou said the King must already know my brother, Charles, is at Vincennes. In that case, perhaps I ought to warn him.

ANNE

Don't be afraid, little one! First of all, this familiar demon of whom I've just heard of for the first time, who's never shown any sign of life, probably exists only in the imagination of Anjou—the wildest of imaginations! Anyway, if Louis knows that the King of England has broken the ban which exiles him from France as it is with my authorization the ban has been lifted, and as Louis only wishes his cousin Charles well—your brother, my child, runs no danger.

HENRIETTE

From my cousin, Louis, no, I know it, but from Cardinal de Mazarin—

ANNE

(with a melancholy smile)

I am forced to confess that the Cardinal, being the friend of Cromwell, is naturally enemies with the King of England.

HENRIETTE

Alas, he's really proved it. My mother hoped that on the death of the Usurper, Cardinal Mazarin would think of my brother,

Charles. The Usurper dies, my brother, Charles, rushes—what's he find? Mr. Richard Cromwell acclaimed, and the Court in mourning for Oliver Cromwell! Oh, Madame isn't it an impiety to see the Court of France in mourning for a man who made his sovereign mount the scaffold, and who, for the last ten years, held the ban of Europe against the legitimate King of England?

ANNE

Hush, my child! All that can change—after days of rain, days of sunshine—! Remember the time when the King, the Duke of Anjou and myself were all dying of hunger at Melun, while you and your mother were dying of hunger at the Louvre—but silence! Mr. de Villeroi is listening to us.

MISS DE LA MOTTE

(linking arms with the Duke d'Anjou)

Milord—repeat to me, I beg you, what the King said just now to Miss Mancini.

D'ANJOU

First of all, he paid her a compliment on her get up—and the fact is it's impossible to have a dress better cut than hers—or which goes badly with the expression on her face.

MISS DE LA MOTTE

I heard he spoke of her eyes—doubtless he said that she had the most magnificent in the world.

D'ANJOU

Right! There won't be enough beautiful words for a bluestocking like the Cardinal's niece—he told her—

(interrupting himself)

Ah, what a charming broach with gemstones you have there.

MISS DE LA MOTTE

Don't you recognize it, Milord?

D'ANJOU

Why indeed! It seems to me I saw it in Louis' hat.

MISS DE LA MOTTE

Don't speak so loud, Milord—you'll make Miss Mancini jealous. He said to her then—about her eyes.

D'ANJOU

That they were deep—like the sea.

MISS DE LA MOTTE

And she replied?

D'ANJOU

And she replied, "Bad comparison, Sire! The sea is treacherous and my eyes never make promises they are not disposed to keep." " They're," replied Louis, "deep like the azure of the heavens which extends above our heads." "Ah," responded Miss Mancini, "I accept that although that azure, may at the moment be torn by some clouds." They are, as you see the most pure and delicate—sheep-like. Ah, indeed—why do you ask me all these questions—Are you no longer amorous of handsome Charmante?

MISS DE LA MOTTE

No more than Miss de Mancini is amorous of the Count de Guiche.

D'ANJOU

Oh! Oh! What's that you're saying beautiful serpent in silk and satin.

MISS DE LA MOTTE

I said that all you need to do to know what's going on is to watch the way the Count de Guiche looks at Miss Mancini and the way Miss Mancini avoids looking at the Count de Guiche.

D'ANJOU

Yes, to realize, that some day the thing between Miss Mancini and the King will end just like the thing between Miss de la Motte and the King ended.

GEORGETTE

(lost behind an armful of bouquets)

Help me! Help me! All my bouquets are going to fall.

LADIES

Ah—charming flowers.

MEN

Oh—pretty girl.

KING

Is it you, Georgette?

D'ANJOU

(low to Marie)

Take care, my lamb! You shed your wool and there are wolves around.

GEORGETTE

Yes, Sire, it's me. Father told me, "Georgette, we mustn't do like the burgomaster, who giving dinner to King Henry IV, kept his good wine for a better occasion. I am going to cut all my flowers, you'll make them into bouquets and take them to the ladies. That will please the King, who is the most gallant gentleman of his court—"

Soon as said, soon as done. Father took his pruning knife, I picked up the flowers and here I am with my bouquets. But I have so many, so many, they are going to fall if no one takes them.

KING

Ladies, you see the situation Georgette's in—be good enough to accept the bouquets that the poor child brings to you. The gardener who gives his flowers, the page who gives his love, the King who gives his crown—are equal before the Lord; Each can only give what he had.

(They relieve Georgette of her bouquets, but she obstinately keeps one.)

GEORGETTE

No, not that one—ladies—no, not that one—gentleman—it's for the King.

(in a low voice)

Or rather for Miss Mancini.

KING

And why is this bouquet for Miss Mancini?

GEORGETTE

Because it is the most beautiful, Sire.

KING

And why must Miss Mancini's bouquet be more beautiful than the other bouquets?

GEORGETTE

Because I was under the table when Mr. de Beringhen told the Queen Mother that Miss Mancini was, since morning, at her window—waiting for you—So, if she was waiting for you at her window all morning, it's because she loves you—and if she loves you—I love her!

KING

Darling little girl! Wait.

(he tears a page from his notebook and writes)

MISS DE LA MOTTE

(who's read what the King wrote, on tiptoe, shrugging)

(aside)

Oh. Indeed I suspected the most beautiful bouquet would be for her.

GEORGETTE

Ah, what you wrote there is very pretty, Sire!

KING

You read it?

GEORGETTE

Yes.

KING

(putting the paper in the bouquet)

Well, now go take this bouquet to Miss Mancini.

GEORGETTE

I'm on my way (low) by the way, Sire, I have something important to tell Your Majesty.

KING

Speak.

GEORGETTE

The Princess Marguerite has just arrived with her mamma and a maid of honor. They will announce Madame Christine under the name of Countess de Verceil.

KING

And how do you know she's Princess Marguerite?

GEORGETTE

I recognized her from the portrait Mr. de Bouchavannes gave you.

KING

Very fine—go!

GEORGETTE

(young to Marie)

Here, Miss—this comes on behalf of the King.

MISS DE LA MOTTE

Ah, Madame, you see it was indeed to her that he wrote.

ANNE

Yes, and you're right, and this very day, I will speak to him about it.

(she gives an order to Beringhen, who then goes to the King)

MARIE

(after having read the letter)

Oh, what charming verse the King sent me, gentlemen. I really told you that he was a poet—listen up:

Go see that object
So sweet and charming
Go little flowers
Die for this beauty
A thousand lovers
Would willingly do more
Who never had
The pleasure you had.

GUICHE

(low)

Marie! Marie!

MARIE

Well, who prevents you from writing poetry to me? No one. It's true, Sire, that you permit Mr. de Guiche, de Villeroi and Dangeau to write me verse—even prettier than this—if they can do so?

KING

Yes, surely I permit it! To prevent them from finding you beautiful, prevent them from telling you so—that would be like forbidding the lark to sing in the morning on the nightingale singing at night—

(Meanwhile the servants have been cleaning up the bottles and the rugs. They've taken down the horn suspended from the branches. Finally a horn—the kill.)

KING

Ladies, you hear? They lanced a beast. To horse, gentlemen—ladies, to horses.

MARIE

Aren't you coming, sire?

KING

No, I am forced to remain a moment for my mother who's making eyes at me. Beringhen has just informed me on her behalf.

MARIE

And about what?

(laughing)

Has the King been disobedient?

KING

It seems that way.

MARIE

And they are going to punish him.

KING

They are going to try to at least.

MARIE

Well—but the hunt?

KING

The trumpets will guide me and I will rejoin it. Meanwhile go there—why not reign where I am not when you already reign where I am?

MARIE

Here's the Queen—be of good cheer, Sire!

KING

The ancient knights fought for their King and for their lady— the King's going to fight for royalty and for you.

ANNE

(going to the King. Mazarin is at the rear talking to a Major Domo, notebook in hand)

You will pardon me, won't you, Louis, to deprive you for a moment of the pleasure of the hunt and the pleasure of accompanying Miss Mancini—but what I have to tell you is truly of the highest importance.

KING

Supposing that a mother who asks for a five minute discussion with her son has need of pardon, you will easily receive mine—for I was determined to remain here for myself—even if I didn't remain here with you and for you.

ANNE

You are staying here?

KING

Yes, I've given a rendezvous to someone, but don't let that annoy you—the person is at my orders and will wait your good pleasure.

ANNE

I thought you too gallant to make a pretty lady wait, Louis.

KING

I'll make all the ladies in the world wait, the most beautiful just like the most powerful, mother, from the moment it's a question of my staying near you—but I don't have even that merit—the person I'm waiting for is not a woman.

ANNE

It's not a woman who's going to come? Why who then is it that you've renounced the hunt to wait for?

KING

Haven't you heard, Madame, what Anjou was saying about a

certain familiar spirit who does me the good office of repeating all that is said and done around me?

ANNE

And since when's this good genie been around you, my son?

KING

Unfortunately for only a short time, Madame—since 11 o'clock this morning.

ANNE

But at 11 o'clock you'd just returned at the Château.

KING

So it was after my return to the Château, Madame, that I had the luck to see him.

ANNE

Impossible! Since 11 o'clock until this very moment, that is to say 2:00 in the afternoon, no strange person has come near you.

KING

(smiling)

To be so sure of what you maintain, Madame, you must also have a familiar spirit who gives you an account of my actions?

ANNE

(without responding)

And this unknown—for he's unknown, doubtless?

KING

To the whole world except me?

ANNE

And this unknown has already returned from where he came?

KING

No, Madame—from today he remains where I am.

ANNE

And what place does he hold at court?

KING

None which may be filled, Madam: That of my friend.

ANNE

He's a gentleman, I presume.

KING

Little matter, Madame! He has no pretention to be present, nor
to ride in my carriage.

ANNE

Take care—you're going to ruffle sensitivities and cause many
complaints.

KING

What sensitivities can be raised by a man who wants to remain invisible? What complaints can be made against an unknown whose main condition of devotion is that he be offered neither place nor offers, nor money.

ANNE

Why then, where's this man dwell?

KING

Outside the palace—he detests the court.

ANNE

Louis, you'll learn eventually that all devotion is paid for and the most disinterested in appearance often ends by being the most costly in reality.

KING

I am sure of few demands from this one.

ANNE

And, doubtless you are also sure of his veracity?

KING

I have irrefutable proof of both, Madame.

ANNE

Really, Louis, I am really crazy to lend myself to a joke, made, doubtless to answer a scatterbrain like d'Anjou, a coquette like Miss Mancini and a ninny like Dangeau—

KING

Pardon, Madame, but you may believe, I beg you that nothing is more real than what I have the honor to tell you at this moment—

ANNE

Truly, you affirm this with a tone—

KING

With a tone of truth, yes, Madame.

ANNE

And since this morning this officious friend has been near you and has already revealed important secrets to you, doubtless?

KING

Only one, Madame, but important enough so that it attracted all my attention.

ANNE

Really?

KING

(taking his mother's arm)

Yes and the discovery of the secret doubled, if that were possible, my respect, my affection, and my gratitude to you, my good mother.

ANNE

In what way?

KING

In proving to me that in my absence as in my presence, far and near, you occupy yourself only with my happiness.

ANNE

Isn't it the first duty of a mother to be concerned about the happiness of her son?

KING

So I'm happy you've furnished me the opportunity to thank you as I do, far from etiquette, one-on-one, your arm leaning on mine, and in an intimacy so rare between these poor folks disinherited from love they call Kings of this earth.

ANNE

You are thanking me, Louis, and I am trying to figure out in what way I've deserved this gratitude.

KING

Look, admit it openly, my good mother, there's a thing you are preoccupied with at this moment, and it was to explain this little matter to me that you asked for this meeting.

ANNE

What are you trying to say?

KING

Of a certain feeling you fear seeing become too tender—

ANNE

You are right; only I don't fear seeing it become too tender; I fear seeing it become too serious.

KING

So be it; but, anyway, I am not mistaken.

ANNE

No. Well?

KING

Well, isn't it in the preoccupation, which indicates, in all respects, your deep tenderness for me, your supreme solicitude for me my renown, that you've come up with the idea of inviting your sister-in-law, Madame Christine de Savoy to come to France under the pretext of those visits paid to close relatives and especially of bringing with her Princess Marguerite, so that the charm of her black eyes may be able to combat the disastrous influence of the blue eyes of Miss Mancini?

ANNE

What! You know—?

KING

I know, Madame, that Princess Marguerite is a worthy grand-daughter of King Henry IV, pious, charitable, enlightened, moreover, a charming person with big melancholy eyes, straight nose, white teeth, olive complexioned—a little dark for those princes like us of the blond race—anyway, I can judge all these matters when I return from the hunt.

ANNE

When you return from the hunt?

KING

Why yes. Don't you know, Madame Christine, accompanies by Princess Marguerite, and a single maid of honor arrived hardly an hour ago at the Château under the name of the Countess de Verceil? Oh truly, Madame, I am very happy to be so well informed that I myself may bring you the first news of an arrival you were awaiting with so much impatience.

ANNE

The Regent and her daughter arrived without my knowing it, after the orders I have given? Impossible and on this point, my son, I am really afraid your secret agent must be at fault.

KING

Well, hold on, Madame, here's Beringhen coming to find you doubtless to confirm what I've had the honor to tell you. Come, Mr. de Beringhen, come—you're looking for the Queen. Here she is.

(He moves away several steps.)

ANNE

(aside)

Ah! Your secret agent! Yes, he really exists, yes, he's quite well informed—but I know who he is, go!

BERINGHEN

Two ladies saying they were invited to France by Your Majesty have just arrived at the Château. The elder of the two calls herself The Countess de Verceil.

ANNE

Who brought this news?

BERINGHEN

A pikeman sent by the Master of Ceremonies, Mr. Montglat. There, Madame, it's the same fellow being questioned at this very moment by Cardinal Mazarin.

ANNE

Let him depart instantly with the order to escort these ladies to the apartments you yourself designated to the upholsterer this morning—which communicates with my room. In a quarter of an hour I will be at Vincennes. Wait for me to accompany me there.

(to Mazarin)

Come, Cardinal.

MAZARIN

It seems, Madame, that our two voyagers have arrived.

(Beringhen goes to the pikeman and orders him to return to the Château. The King remains at the back.)

ANNE

Yes.

(pointing to the King)

You've told him everything, sir!

MAZARIN

First all, Majesty, I never say anything.

ANNE

And still he's aware of it.

MAZARIN

I assure you, Madame, that I don't know what you mean.

ANNE

I am speaking of the King, sir, and I tell you he knows every-thing.

MAZARIN

What do you call knowing everything, dear Majesty?

ANNE

He knows that I distrust his new love, he knows my plan to unite him to Princess Marguerite, he knows what I myself didn't know—that the two princesses have arrived.

MAZARIN

Egad—he knows that, Majesty! And who could tell him?

ANNE

Then, Cardinal, pardon me this nasty thought if it is false, but I imagine that as you are more interested that anyone that this marriage not take place, it was you, who, to ruin it, told everything to the King.

MAZARIN

More interested than anyone? I don't understand Your Majesty.

ANNE

Doubtless! The King—

MAZARIN

The King—

ANNE

Isn't the King in love with your niece?

MAZARIN

You think so? Oh!

ANNE

I'm bringing you the news, right, Cardinal?

MAZARIN

You know that is the custom of His Majesty to find love in my family—and that those loves are without importance.

ANNE

Yes, I know it, but if his new love became more serious than the other? If he wanted to make Marie what he lacked the courage to make Olympia?

MAZARIN

Well, we'd marry the little one with some prince of the blood of France or Savoy just as we already married three of her sisters.

ANNE

Marry her to whom you like, Cardinal, but there's one thing I promise you—she won't marry the King.

MAZARIN

Eh! Egad, who's thinking of such an enormity? The King perhaps, but not me, for sure!

ANNE

Listen, sir—I don't think the King is capable of such baseness, but if it's possible that he even thought of it, I warn you that all France would revolt against him and against you, that I would place myself at the head of the revolt, and that if need be, I would enlist my second son in it! Come, Beringhen.

(She leaves.)

KING

(to himself)

Good! It seems the news had produced its effect.

MAZARIN

(aside)

Ah, you'll place yourself at the head of the revolt and you'll involve your other son in it? That would not prevent it if the King absolutely insists on being the nephew of Cardinal Mazarin—he'll do to his mommy, to the revolt of the Duke d'Anjou, what he did to the Parliament this morning—and as for me, as I am his subject, if he said to me, 'My dear Cardinal, I wish to marry your niece' I couldn't disobey him by refusing her to him—this cherished King!

KING

(coming forward)

Ah! My God! What's the matter with my mother, my dear Cardinal? She's getting into her carriage growling like a thunderstorm.

MAZARIN

Eh! Sire, who knows that's the matter with a woman especially when that woman is Queen?

KING

It's not with me she's angry, I hope, Mr. Mazarin—right?

MAZARIN

No.

KING

Anyway, as I have something to ask—it is true, but not of her— her good or ill humor doesn't matter much.

MAZARIN

(sweetly)

You have something to ask of someone, my dear King?

KING

Yes.

MAZARIN

Of whom?

KING

Of you.

MAZARIN

Ask, my dear child, ask! Oh, pardon, pardon, Sire! There I go speaking to Your Majesty like in those days when the Queen Mother was regent and King Louis was a little boy no higher than that.

KING

Eh? Don't you still have the right to speak to me that way, my dear Cardinal? Who raised me? You! Who followed me into exile? You! Who protected me? You! If I am King of France, is it not because of you I am, and if, after God, I must owe my kingdom to someone, isn't it to you I owe it?

MAZARIN

Are you really convinced of what you are saying to me Louis?

KING

Why that's history Cardinal Mazarin.

MAZARIN

Oh—history is sometimes such a liar—and you were telling me, my dear child, that you had something to ask of me. Look, what is it? Speak.

KING

Yes, but before making this request to you, I want to ask you a question?

MAZARIN

What?

KING

Are you a good mood at the moment, my dear Cardinal?

MAZARIN

Today?

KING

Yes, today.

MAZARIN

Today, I am in a charming mood!

(he smiles at the King, who puts his arm through his—just as with his mother)

KING

Well, my dear Cardinal, I need money.

MAZARIN

(pulling back)

Money?

KING

Yes, money.

MAZARIN

Pardon, Sire, I was hoping to have heard badly. Money! And what do you want to do with money?

KING

Why give balls, parties, spectacles—in the end to amuse myself.

MAZARIN

Amuse yourself, Sire! Do you think one is King to amuse oneself?

KING

My dear Cardinal, a King must either amuse himself or reign—now, at the moment you and my mother reign—so it's necessary I amuse myself. If not, take care! I might notice I am not reigning.

MAZARIN

(aside)

Wow! What's he saying?

KING

That's why I am asking for money.

MAZARIN

Money! Money! Word of honor, you'd say the royal vocabulary was composed of those two words, money. The Queen asks for it in her sharp voice, "Money, Cardinal!" The Duke d'Anjou asks for it in his sweet voice, 'Cardinal, money!'. The King asks for it—but Sire! There is no money. I've put all that we had into this party—I've just gone through the calculations with the Major Domo—it's costing 500 crowns.

KING

Well then, my dear Mr. Mazarin, as I am very bored, and there's no money, so it seems—

MAZARIN

No—Sire—there's no money.

KING

Then to distract myself, I'll have to mix in affairs of state. It's not amusing, but after all, it's still a distraction. You will tell, I beg you, Mr. Fouquet, Mr. Lyonne and Mr. Tellier to come work with me tomorrow instead of going to work with you. During that time, you will not work, my dear Cardinal. After thirty years of your life dedicated to France, you surely must need a lot of rest—while after six years of vacation, I must need some work.

MAZARIN

(rubbing his ear)

And you need a great deal of money my dear King?

KING

No—

MAZARIN

Oh, why if it's a little sum—there's a way to get on.

KING

A little sum—for a King—especially when he has such rich ministers around him.

MAZARIN

Oh—yes, Mr. Fouquet—it's a scandal. Why, let's see—the total of—you understand—everything depends on the total—

KING

Well, I think with a million—

MAZARIN

(starting)

A million?

KING

Yes, I'll spend the season hunting.

MAZARIN

One million—my dear Loulon—

KING

Do you think it too little for a king of France?

MAZARIN

A million, my dear child! But where do you think I'll get a million?

KING

Why? It seemed to me, sir, that from the moment I registered the decrees of Parliament—

MAZARIN

Oh, Sire! First they must be promulgated, published, put into execution, and consequently, before the money starts coming in, more than a year will pass—more than two years—even then it may never come in—that rascally money! The unhappy people are so wretched—so ruined—so poor—ah!

KING

Well, my dear Cardinal, while waiting for the money to come in, couldn't you lend me that money?

MAZARIN

Jesus!

KING

You'll get it back from the first taxes which will pour into the treasury.

MAZARIN

Me, Sire, me—lend you a million?

KING

Why, yes—nothing would be easier for you.

MAZARIN

Madonna! And where do you think I would get it—this money?

KING

Why, for example—hold on, my dear Cardinal—try the three million nine hundred thousand pounds—from Lyon or the seven million in Bordeaux—or the four million in Madrid.

MAZARIN

Christ Jesus!

KING

Or indeed, if you hesitate to withdraw money so advantageously placed, which is conceivable, borrow the sum on your nine millions or real estate—I'll pay interest at 10 percent.

MAZARIN

I am robbed, betrayed, ruined.

KING

Or indeed couldn't you spare this million from your seven millions of general income? What do I know about it? Finally, it seems to me my dear Cardinal, that a minister who possesses so much money in properties and cash receipts, 39 million two hundred thousand pounds could readily lend a million to his King—

MAZARIN

Why, who told you this—who could have told you?

KING

The same person who informed of the trip to France of Madame Christine and Princess Marguerite: My secret agent.

MAZARIN

But—it's that the figure is so exact.

KING

My agent is incapable of being misled even about a penny.

MAZARIN

And when must you have this million, Sire?

KING

This evening, my dear Cardinal.

MAZARIN

But what do you want to do with a million?

KING

Listen—I'm going to tell you this—because for you to whom I owe so much I have no secrets, I'm in love.

MAZARIN

You're in love!

KING

And I absolutely will please the woman I love.

MAZARIN

And you absolutely will please her?

KING

Yes.

MAZARIN

Oh, a King as charming as you are has no need of a million to make a woman mad for him.

KING

No matter, my dear Cardinal, a million spent on parties of which she will be the queen won't be ill spent. I am sure of it.

MAZARIN

Of which she will be the Queen? Ah, my dear King, so you intend to make the one you love Queen?

KING

Of my parties, my dear Cardinal, meanwhile, perhaps she may be Queen of the Realm.

MAZARIN

Since you give such good reasons, we'll do our utmost—we will hasten the income from taxes, we'll pursue contributions.

KING

And I shall have the million tonight?

MAZARIN

What do you mean tonight?

KING

My dear Cardinal, my love is so great that it admits of no delay.

MAZARIN

Ah! If your love is so great, that's another matter—well—

KING

Well—

MAZARIN

(with a sigh)

We'll try to give you this wretched million!

KING

Truly, you are a charming man, my dear Cardinal.

(going towards the back)

MAZARIN

The King's going.

KING

Yes—wait, they're sounding the Haloo a hundred paces from here, and I am going to reach the hunt.

(Exit the King.)

MAZARIN

(alone)

Till tonight, my dear King! My dear child, my dear nephew. Ah, you're in love! Ah! You want to make the woman you love queen of your parties—and perhaps Queen of your realm! May God hear you! I've got an idea who played me this dirty touch of giving him this devilish total—ah, Madame Anne of Austria, Anne of Austria! You will pay me for this.

BERNOUIN

(entering)

Ah! There's Milord—Milord!

MAZARIN

What? Ah, it's you Bernouin! Come, my dear Bernouin, come my friend, come!

BERNOUIN

Oh, oh, what's the matter with Your Eminence—you seem very agitated to me.

MAZARIN

Yes—tormented, my dear Bernouin—and full of joy, too—a bit—but what's going on down there that brings you here? I told you not to rejoin me unless something important happened.

BERNOUIN

Two important things, Milord.

MAZARIN

Ah, two?

BERNOUIN

Yes, two big events. First of all, Mr. de Conti is at Vincennes to bring to the King, the Submission of the Prince de Condé.

MAZARIN

And the other?

BERNOUIN

And to announce that Prince Condé is ill in Brussels.

MAZARIN

Ah! Poor Prince—he's ill?

BERNOUIN

Very ill, Milord—which makes him wish to return to France and therefore he sends his submission.

MAZARIN

I will send him Guenaud, my doctor. And one mustn't forget in the last analysis—he's a prince of the blood.

BERNOUIN

And as for his return to France?

MAZARIN

If he's as sick as you say, Bernouin, he has more need of a doctor than a passport—and it would be to risk his health to permit him to set out on a trip. No, Guenaud will cure him first—that will take time—and during that time, I will consider—Bernouin, if ever you became a statesman never forget that the great secret of politics is: Know when to wait—the other event, Bernouin?

BERNOUIN

The other event, Milord, is the presence of King Charles II at Vincennes.

MAZARIN

King Charles II is at Vincennes?

BERNOUIN

Yes.

MAZARIN

Are you sure of this?

BERNOUIN

I am sure of it.

MAZARIN

Who saw him?

BERNOUIN

I did, behind a window blind at the hotel Crowned Peacock, near the parade ground.

MAZARIN

Ah, Bernouin, yes, you are right—this is great event! It's Anne of Austria who's brought things to this muddle—as if things weren't muddled enough already. Ah, if King Charles the II were on the throne of England, I think that little Henriette, rather than the Infanta, would be the wife for the King and we would be marrying a great power at least—! But it's Mr. Richard Cromwell, who, for the moment is King of England and we have to deal with him—Bernouin, you're going to return to the Château and send Guitaut to me when you arrive—do you hear?

BERNOUIN

What! You are going to arrest King Charles II?

MAZARIN

Oh, no! One must have respect for crowned heads. I am going to order him to leave France in a week—and Vincennes in twenty-four hours.

BERNOUIN

And if he won't leave?

MAZARIN

Then it won't be my fault, it will be his. I will act.

BERNOUIN

Hum!

MAZARIN

Bernouin! If ever you are a minister, remember to treat everything with these words: Know when to act.

BERNOUIN

How does Milord reconcile this second maxim with the first?

MAZARIN

I don't reconcile them; I put them face to face—I interchange them, and according to the occasion I use the one I have need of. But hush!

BERNOUIN

What?

MAZARIN

Do you see who's coming over there?

BERNOUIN

Ah! Ah! His Majesty and Miss Mancini.

MAZARIN

Return to Vincennes and warn Doctor Guenaud to be prepared
to leave.

BERNOUIN

Yes, Milord.

MAZARIN

Don't tell him for what country.

BERNOUIN

Have no fear.

MAZARIN

Warn Guitaut to be ready to act.

BERNOUIN

Yes, Milord.

MAZARIN

Don't tell him against who!

BERNOUIN

Don't worry.

MAZARIN

Go.

(Bernouin leaves, the Cardinal leaves in his turn at the moment the King and Marie enter.)

MARIE

I hope, Sire, that they don't make a stag who is a better courtier than ours—he saw the King didn't want to take the trouble of running after him and he returned politely to die by your lance—Ah, animals sometimes give men really bad examples.

KING

You think so? It's possible—but let's leave stags, hunting dogs, huntsmen, horns and fanfares—come over this way, Marie, I need to be alone a moment with you, to hear your sweet voice, apart from other voices, to see your charming face in a mirror in which it alone is reflected—you are like the good fairies, who with a touch of their golden wand—chase off ghosts and make evil spirits disappear.

(The wind comes up and the weather darkens.)

MARIE

Oh, Sire, what a beautiful place, Your Majesty gives me near the King.

KING

Marie, do you know anything sweeter than that of a woman who makes a King forget the cares of royalty?

MARIE

But, above all things, the woman must be loved and be especially certain of it.

KING

And what must that prince do to prove his love to her?

MARIE

One of the first things would be when, where she's hunting to follow the hunt rather than to send her to the other end of the forest to remain alone—for what purpose? God only knows!

KING

By chance would I have the great good fortune to be making you jealous, dearest Marie?

MARIE

If it were a great good fortune to you, Sire, it would be a great misfortune for me!

KING

Why's that? And how could my good fortune cause misfortune to you? You are always talking to me about my power, of my scepter, of my crown. Alas, the only true royal crown that God puts on the head of his elect is that of love. All the others bridle or burn the face of those that wear them. Love alone lights and rejuvenates it.

MARIE

Well, Sire, who told you that the woman to whom you may give this crown, if you asked frankly, and in a bold voice—who told you she would refuse it?

KING

Yes, but who tells me that it would really be to the lover and not the King that this crown were given?

(Rain falls, the king sheltering Marie with is hat, leads her under the oak of Saint Louis. The other hunters reappear, but noticing the King and Marie don't dare approach their horses and carriages—and remain hesitating at the distance for the remainder of the act.)

KING

What says that an ambitious love wouldn't sacrifice some tender passion, the more enviable in its obscurity, in its mystery, in its tenderness than that seen in full daylight? There are moments when, instead of being born on the throne, I would be born the least of my subjects, for then if a young and beautiful mouth like yours said to me "Louis, I love you" I would be really sure of being loved.

MARIE

Eh! Do you think, Sire, that the woman who loves you, for her part, won't be tormented by the same fears that torment you? If you were the last of your subjects, if you were miserable, if you were poor, she who was offering to share your poverty and your misery would know her devotion could be compensation; that a minister wouldn't shout, "Sire, reason of state!" That a mother wouldn't say, "My son, pride of blood." To love an ordinary man,

Sire, is to be the companion of his entire life—to love a King is to be the mistress of a day, the fantasy of an hour, the caprice of a moment—it's to do what we are both doing, here under this oak which lightning may strike; It's to forget the weather which grows gloomy, the thunder which roars, the rain which falls—to enjoy an hour of happiness which perhaps won't last any longer than this passing lightening! Oh—the woman who feels herself disposed to love a king, a young king, powerful like you—such a woman, if she had the light of reason in her mind, a shred of decency in her soul, that woman, rather than let her love grow, rather than let herself be dominated by it, would search it out in the deepest recesses of her heart and choke it pitilessly with both her hands.

(Mazarin appears in the grotto listening.)

KING

And what tells you, Marie, that if the King was sure of this love, he would not care that the woman who gave it to him wasn't a princess, a King's daughter, a queen's sister? Is it absolutely necessary to maintain the grandeur of state to safeguard the dignity of the crown?—that the heart be sacrificed eternally to the exigencies of politics? What does it matter to the prosperity of France that I marry some poor Princess from Savoy, Portugal, Germany or the woman I love? That I be wretched in my majesty or happy in my love? Listen carefully here, Marie, I am king resolutely determined to tell whoever crosses my plans henceforth what I told Parliament this morning. 'It is my will.' I am King, I say—and minister, mother, France, Europe will bend before my sovereign unchangeable will! Oh—let her love me, let her love me alone! Then I feel that this love is powerful— deep, eternal, that the woman who lives me with a love equal to mine will be pure, young, beautiful, that this woman be like you—Marie—and I will say to this woman: 'Here's my heart!' and I will say to France: 'Here's your Queen!'"

MARIE

Oh, Sire! Sire! If one could believe such a promise it would drive a woman who loved you crazy! But no, no! Miss de la Motte loved you!

MARIE

She had a husband!

MARIE

My sister, Olympia loved you.

KING

I was a child.

MARIE

Miss de la Motte loved you.

KING

I didn't love her!

MARIE

But me, but me, Sire! Oh! My God! My God!

KING

You, Marie! You are another matter.

(thunder rolls)

As for you, I love you.

(falling to his knees)

MARIE

(joyfully and dazzled)

Ah!

(getting control of herself, and looking in the distance)

Sire, in the name of heaven, get up! Shut up! They're looking at us, they hear us! They're listening to us.

KING

Eh! Who cares! Take my arm, Marie—and raise your head!

(to hunters)

Gentlemen, we can return to our carriages—I think the storm is over and that the thunder abates.

D'ANJOU

Yes, brother, at the feet of Marie Mancini, abating and saying to you, 'I love you!'

MAZARIN

(leaving the grotto and observing the King and Marie)

Come, I think my million will return to me many times over.

CURTAIN

ACT III

Mazarin's apartment. In the rear, Mazarin's bedroom—in the foreground a first class room with three doors and a window.

MAZARIN

(coming from the bedchamber, leaning on Guenaud's arm)

You understand, Guenaud. Leave this moment! The Prince Condé is very ill! Cure him, Guenaud, not too quickly—rapid cures are not certain—you have leave for a month—even two months. You understand.

GUENAUD

Understand perfectly, Milord.

MAZARIN

And I'll have news of the Prince.

GUENAUD

Whenever you wish.

MAZARIN

I want it every day, Guenaud.

GUENAUD

But what about you, during this time, Milord?

MAZARIN

Don't you worry about me, my dear Guenaud! I never felt so well in my life! Go, Guenaud, go, my friend!

(alone)

Good! During the two months which the convalescence of the Prince Condé will last, I'll have time to receive news from Spain, and according as God decides there, we shall act here.

BERNOUIN

(entering)

Milord.

MAZARIN

It's you, Bernouin?

BERNOUIN

Yes, Milord.

(low)

Mr. Guitaut is here.

MAZARIN

Ah, that good Guitaut—show him in, Bernouin. You know how much I like him.

(Bernouin exits and returns with Guitaut.)

GUITAUT

Hello, Milord. Your Eminence has something to ask of me?

MAZARIN

Yes, I have several things to tell you.

GUITAUT

Tell me, Milord!

MAZARIN

First, you never speak to me enough of your nephew, Comingues.

GUITAUT

My nephew, Comingues is always your servant and that of the Queen, Milord. Who must be arrested?

MAZARIN

(pretending not to understand him)

You still get news of him, don't you?

GUITAUT

By each courier who comes from Portugal, yes, Milord—Look, it is a professional, a churchman, or a gentleman?

MAZARIN

(without answering)

I thought it was a question of a marriage between him and your charming daughter. You know, Mr. Guitaut, that in the case that marriage took place, the King would give him a hundred thousand crowns and would sign the contract?

GUITAUT

That would be great, Milord, for up until now, we'd received more kicks than crowns in the royal service. Where's the arrest warrant?

MAZARIN

You think it's a question of arresting someone, my dear Guitaut?

GUITAUT

By God! When they make you Captain of the Guards, when they promise your daughter one hundred thousand crowns—

(aside)

which will never be paid

(aloud)

They need a captain of the guards.

MAZARIN

Well, yes, I have need of you, Guitaut, but you are mistaken, it's not to arrest someone.

GUITAUT

Oh! Oh! What has to be done?

MAZARIN

It's to tell a foreigner who's bedding at the Hotel Crowned Peacock that I know he's there—

GUITAUT

Fine! You know he's there—and you wish—

MAZARIN

I want him to leave the hotel.

GUITAUT

And can he lodge in some other place in Vincennes, Milord?

MAZARIN

What I want is for him to leave not only the hotel but Vincennes, too—if it's not too unpleasant for him.

GUITAUT

Good! And he can return to Paris, then?

MAZARIN

Bah! Paris is too near Vincennes, Guitaut and I want him to leave Paris, as well—if that doesn't cause him too much trouble.

GUITAUT

And in what corner of France will he be allowed to live?

MAZARIN

Ah! I'd really like him to leave France, too—if that wouldn't cause him too much displeasure.

GUITAUT

Meaning you exile him—?

MAZARIN

Eh! My God, no! I'm sending him back where he comes from, that's all.

GUITAUT

And if he refuses?

MAZARIN

If he refuses?

GUITAUT

Yes.

MAZARIN

Then you understand, Guitaut, it would be different—we'd have to use force—but with the greatest care—

GUITAUT

Ah, indeed—why then he's a great lord?

MAZARIN

A very great lord, Guitaut!

GUITAUT

Much greater than Mr. de Longueville?

MAZARIN

Much greater!

GUITAUT

Greater than the Prince de Condé?

MAZARIN

Much greater still!

GUITAUT

Much greater than Mr. de Beaufort?

MAZARIN

Still much greater!

GUITAUT

Why, he's a king then?

MAZARIN

He's a king and he's not a king—you understand, Guitaut?

GUITAUT

No, I don't understand.

MAZARIN

In your opinion is it might or right that makes a King?

GUITAUT

It's right, Milord.

MAZARIN

Well, as for me, I am not at all of your opinion. Therefore, Mr. Richard Cromwell, to my eyes, is the true King of England until Mr. Monk decides otherwise.

GUITAUT

Ah, Milord, then it's King Charles who's involved?

MAZARIN

Exactly, you see then, Guitaut that I cannot recommend you too much attentiveness, care, politeness for, indeed King Charles II is the grandson of Henry IV of France. The nephew of Queen Anne of Austria, the cousin of the King! So you will make him mount a good carriage harnessed with excellent horses—you will get in after him, you will sit by his side on his left, you do understand, Guitaut? One mustn't be lacking in etiquette with a Majesty—! And you will place gentle officers—good gentleman—the most lovable you can find on the seat facing him—and in that way, you'll escort him to the border with Holland, Guitaut.

GUITAUT

But the King? But the Queen?

MAZARIN

Unnecessary to tell them anything—it would pain them.

GUITAUT

Do you know what they're saying about the King?

MAZARIN

No—

GUITAUT

Impossible?

MAZARIN

I am not curious.

GUITAUT

Well, they say about the King that clever as you may be, Milord, you can hide nothing that you are doing from him.

MAZARIN

And you believe that, Guitaut? Oh!

GUITAUT

That he has a secret agent, thanks to whom no mysteries exist for him any more!

MAZARIN

About the court, Guitaut!

GUITAUT

I tell you for what it's worth, Milord, it's proved to me that you are minister—it's not proven to me that the King may be King—the arrest warrant comes to me from you; I will execute it—where is it?

MAZARIN

Here it is in writing, Guitaut. But with the greatest delicacy, you understand, Guitaut?

GUITAUT

Yes, Milord.

MAZARIN

To his left, Guitaut, to his left and always 'Majesty'.

GUITAUT

Don't worry.

MAZARIN

Go, my friend, go!

(Guitaut leaves by the door opposite the one Guenaud left by.)

MAZARIN

(alone)

This dear Guitaut. There's a faithful servant—never argues, always ready to execute. Ah, these Guitauts are ruining themselves. Good family, all the same good blood. But if this devil of a rumor should spread that the King knows all the court secrets—Eh! Eh!

MARIE

(by the door)

Can one come in, my dear uncle?

MAZARIN

I think so, indeed! A ray of sun after the cloud. Come in, my little Marie, come in.

MARIE

Oh, how good you are to me this evening, my dear uncle.

MAZARIN

Do you know something, Marie? It's that of all my nieces—and God be thanked! I am not short of them—it's that of all my nieces, you are the one I love the most.

MARIE

Really, my uncle? But why have you kept this secret from me for seventeen years?

MAZARIN

I didn't want to excite jealousy.

MARIE

Well, uncle, as for me, I guessed this tenderness, so will hidden though it was—and I loved you, on my part, as if you'd shown me preference.

MAZARIN

And then, I didn't want to give you too much pride in letting you see all the good things I thought of you—you see, little one, pride is a mortal sin—as I always told myself watching your sisters grow and flourish—"Let them be flirts, it's my little Marie who will be the honor and the glory of the house!"

MARIE

And you think the predicted hour has come, uncle?

MAZARIN

I think it's approaching! This morning even, I was speaking with Bernouin about you, and I told him, "The others, they'll marry counts, dukes, princes of the blood—and I won't be satisfied until I've married Marie to a King."

MARIE

To a king?

MAZARIN

Yes—I still don't know who yet, but I won't be satisfied, I repeat, until I've married you to a king.

MARIE

Do you know your prejudice in my favor makes you highly ambitious, uncle?

MAZARIN

Why? Aren't you as beautiful as a royal princess? And if there was around that neck a diamond necklace, and diamond earrings on those ears, and on that head a diadem of diamonds—wouldn't you look as Queenly as that little she-hen from Savoy that they want to marry the King?

MARIE

Yes, uncle, I would be—but on this neck, these ears, this head, there are only the simple graces that nature has around them—graces, my uncle, that in my favor and prejudice have always been found sufficient.

MAZARIN

Well, Miss Mancini, as for me, I am going to prove to you that you are an ingrate.

(calling)

Bernouin! Bernouin!

BERNOUIN

(appearing)

Milord!

MAZARIN

Give me the little jewel box I told you to bring from Paris and that I intended—for whom did I intend it, Bernouin?

BERNOUIN

For Miss Marie Mancini.

MAZARIN

Go, Bernouin.

(Bernouin leaves)

There, you see, I didn't make him say it—that dear Bernouin! He betrays my weakness—but with good intention.

BERNOUIN

(returning with the jewel box)

Here, Milord.

MAZARIN

(taking it in his hands)

You know, my little Marie, I've always loved precious stones, but in particular, I prefer the diamond—that's the most costly and most rare—the only one that truly is like a sun's ray.

(pulling diamonds from the box)

These diamonds—they're my sun, mine—a poor slave of politics who for the last sixteen years led a wearisome life. These diamonds, often, at night after a rough day—or in the morning when one night had been bad—well, I made them bring them to me in my bed—I spread them out on silk lace, I looked at them, I rubbed them, I polished them , and they rejoiced me—I know them by sight. Well, these diamonds, each time that I see them, I tell myself "These diamonds, one day, they'll be for my little Marie."

MARIE

Really, uncle, you said that?

MAZARIN

Yes, and you would have had them already if it weren't so hard for me to part with them.

MARIE

What you mean is you love your diamonds more than you love me.

MAZARIN

Oh!

MARIE

Come on—admit it.

MAZARIN

Why no, since today to make you more beautiful than the little Savoyard who comes from Turin, from Cambery, I don't know where—! Since today—but you'll promise me to be more beautiful than she, won't you?

MARIE

Oh, I swear to you, uncle, I'll do all I can and if I fail it won't be my fault.

MAZARIN

Well, these diamonds, that until today I've only entrusted to Bernouin, are worth a hundred thousand crowns—to make you pretty—prettier than Princess Marguerite today—I—I—my little Marie—today—take special care of them—I'm loaning them to you.

(he leaves)

MARIE

(laughing)

Oh—he's loaning them to me! My uncle makes the supreme effort to loan me these diamonds, do you understand Bernouin? That astonishes me, as much as if he had given them to me.

BERNOUIN

Take them anyway, Miss, and don't trouble yourself about the rest.

MARIE

But you heard, Bernouin? He said, "I'm loaning them to you."

BERNOUIN

Miss, I've been near His Eminence for thirty years and after thirty years I've heard him say only three times, "I am loaning you" and once "I am giving you" and that time was the evening he gave to Madame Tubouef—who just brought him the ten thousand pounds that her husband had lost in gambling against him that night. I will say to you as the Cardinal said to her "Make yourself beautiful, Miss! Make yourself beautiful!"

(he leaves)

MARIE

Oh! Yes, yes, I understand what you mean, my uncle, and what your faithful Bernouin says after you. You weren't so well concealed that I didn't notice you, during the storm—in that grotto—in the forest of Vincennes! You saw the King at my feet—and look where your ambition has taken your avarice. When the King paid no attention to me, I was indifferent to you—the King looks at me, I am pretty; the King loves me; you adore me! Oh—you're right uncle, and it was I who was wrong to listen to a simple gentleman like Mr. Guiche. But who could suspect that the King of France, that Louis XIV would pay attention to me? Who in my isolation found myself very happy to be loved by the handsomest gentleman of the Court! Yes, but while waiting, how imprudent I've been! Oh, but when

I appeal to his—delicacy when he understands it's a question not of being the mistress of the King of France, but of being Queen of France—he'll get out of my path, he'll leave the court. "Make yourself beautiful! Make yourself beautiful!" Well, since the whole world wants it—let's try.

(sits on the stool in the middle of the stage and opens the box)

Oh, what magnificent diamonds.

D'ANJOU

(who's coming in on tiptoe, and looking over his shoulder)

Oh—What magnificent diamonds!

MARIE

(turning)

Huh!

D'ANJOU

Have no fear—the nymph Echo is here!

MARIE

Oh—why look, Milord! Look.

D'ANJOU

I see indeed—but who gave you all this?

MARIE

My uncle!

D'ANJOU

What uncle? You've got two uncles?

MARIE

My uncle, Mazarin.

D'ANJOU

Can't be true.

MARIE

(laughing)

Oh—oh—a lie, Milord!

D'ANJOU

But you know quite well yourself that it's not possible.

MARIE

Still it is.

D'ANJOU

Oh—never mind—wherever they come from show them to me, dear Marie.

MARIE

I will do better than say to you 'look', Milord—I say to you, 'take.'

D'ANJOU

Really, you offer this like a baptismal bonbon.

MARIE

Why not, since I am a godmother.

D'ANJOU

Whose relative?

MARIE

Of the generosity of Cardinal Mazarin, who just gave birth after fifty years pregnancy—the father is ill, but the baby is doing fine.

D'ANJOU

Oh—I'm there?

MARIE

What?

D'ANJOU

My brother's secret agent told him Mazarin had millions stuffed in his cellars—and our dear Cardinal, who fears to have them taken from him, is trying to save something from the fire.

MARIE

That may be the reason—or another—little matter—we've got the jewel box—that's the main thing.

D'ANJOU

Oh, but look—what a hat braid that string of diamonds would make.

MARIE

Look at this necklace, what an admirable choker.

D'ANJOU

And this cloak clasp.

MARIE

And these earrings.

D'ANJOU

And these cuff buttons.

MARIE

And this diadem of gems.

D'ANJOU

But look, Marie!

MARIE

But see, Prince!

(Each one fumbles in the box and takes something out with exclamations of joy.)

KING

(appearing in the doorway and seeing them both resplendent with jewels)

Why goodness—have they stolen the crown treasure here?

MARIE

Ah! The king.

(she takes the box and runs off)

KING

Marie! Marie!

D'ANJOU

The box! The box!

KING

She's run off—she's fleeing me! Do you understand this d'Anjou?

D'ANJOU

Indeed, I do! You came suddenly without having yourself

announced, before the sun had time to light all its rays: The sun hid itself! Oh, but don't worry—it won't delay reappearing—go! and more resplendent than ever.

KING

And what were the two of you doing?

D'ANJOU

We were selecting Mazarin's diamonds.

KING

I don't understand.

D'ANJOU

I imagine you don't! Listen Louis, and attend to an incredible unheard of exorbitant news—Mazarin has become generous.

KING

Liar!

D'ANJOU

Mazarin just gave Marie a a hundred thousand crowns worth of diamonds.

KING

They were fake then?

D'ANJOU

Here, look—see—I said just like you, at first, I screamed "It's not true, it's impossible" but then I discovered the secret—brother we were mistaken—Mazarin is a prodigal—and it doesn't—it won't astonish me that he will profit by my being here to make me some magnificent gift—eh! Right, here's Bernouin.

BERNOUIN

The King.

KING

Come on in, Bernouin, come on in!

BERNOUIN

The King will excuse me, but I've come for the Duke.

D'ANJOU

You see! What is it Bernouin?

BERNOUIN

His Eminence having learned from Miss Mancini that Milord was here, begs His Highness to accept, as pocket money and to cut a figure gambling three thousand crowns—

D'ANJOU

Where's it, Bernouin?

BERNOUIN

In this purse.

D'ANJOU

Well, what was I telling you, brother! Gimme, Bernouin, gimme.

(emptying the purse into his hat)

What—this is for me, and this here gold?

BERNOUIN

Yes, Milord.

D'ANJOU

(giving a fistful of gold to Bernouin)

Here Bernouin, this is for you. Want some, Louis?

BERNOUIN

I thank Milord very much.

D'ANJOU

(to king)

Oh, take it, take it, don't trouble yourself, when I am rich, it's to give.

BERNOUIN

It's useless for Milord to deprive himself in favor of the King, his brother. I was ordered by His Majesty to go to the King and remit to him this purse which contains a million.

KING

Thanks, Bernouin.

D'ANJOU

Diamonds for Marie, three thousand crowns for me! A million for you! All this coming from the Cardinal.

(calling)

Doctor Guenaud! Doctor Guenaud!

BERNOUIN

What are you doing, Milord?

D'ANJOU

I'm calling the doctor. Oh, what a misfortune, Bernouin—the Cardinal is mad—Guenaud! Guenaud!

(he gambols out, rattling his coins, calling "Guenaud!")

GEORGETTE

(at the window) (outside)

Who called for Mr. Guenaud? Was it you, Sire?

KING

No—it's not me, Georgette.

BERNOUIN

The King has no orders to give me?

KING

Tell His Eminence I thank him, and that soon, at the gaming table, I will thank him again.

(Bernouin bows and leaves.)

GEORGETTE

Ah—if you want Doctor Guenaud, Sire, it won't do you any good to call him—because he won't come.

KING

And why's that?

GEORGETTE

Because he's no longer here.

KING

Bah?

GEORGETTE

No, he left for a long long trip.

KING

So where'd he go?

GEORGETTE

To Brussels in Brabant to care for Prince Condé who is ill.

KING

Prince Condé is ill? And who told you that, Georgette? Come, tell me about this, come—!

(helps her in the window)

GEORGETTE

No one told me, but I heard. The horse of Doctor Guenaud was tied to the gate of the park, and I was feeding him a handful of green hay when I saw Dr. Guenaud and Mr. Molière come— they were talking together heatedly. Mr. Molière said, 'But the King is not going to allow Prince Condé to reenter France?" Dr. Guenaud replied, "Right! The King, who knows everything doesn't even know that Condé has made his submission!" "Why didn't Condé directly petition the King instead of Cardinal Mazarin?" said Molière, "The King has a great heart whereas Cardinal Mazarin has only servants." "Oh," replied Dr. Guenaud "because Prince Condé knows that the King doesn't meddle in affairs of state, he has enough to do meddling in love affairs!" "Oh, if I dared" replied Molière, "I would myself speak to him about it, and I am sure that, if I told him about this, all that I am going to tell him—the King, rather than get angry with me, would be pleased by my frankness." It was then they said Prince Condé was in a town called Brussels in Brabant and the Doctor added that was where he was going and that it was necessary that the Prince's convalescence last two months—etc., etc.

KING

Georgette, I promise you that I won't leave Vincennes without having found you a husband and giving you a dowry.

GEORGETTE

What'll I do with that?

KING

What'll you do with a dowry?

GEORGETTE

No—with a husband.

KING

Why, get married, it seems to me—

GEORGETTE

(unenthusiastic)

Thanks, Sire.

KING

(surprised)

What do you mean, "thanks"?

GEORGETTE

I don't want to get married!

KING

You don't want to get married?

GEORGETTE

No.

KING

What do you want to do?

GEORGETTE

I want to be an actress.

KING

An actress! Eh, Good God! How did you get such an idea, Georgette?

GEORGETTE

Oh, quite naturally, Sire. My father took me to the theater twice, once at the Hotel Bourgogne, and once at the Comedy Italian— that gave me the folly.

KING

Ah! That's the source of your ruin! And you think you are going to act like that, right away—first try?

GEORGETTE

Oh, it's not really difficult to act! I'll do the way I've seen it done. At the Hotel de Bourgogne there was a lady with feathers in her hair, a big cloak of silk with gold brocade and a brocade dress—who was by herself—her arms folded and she said:

(declaiming)

"At last, cowardly emperor! I perceive your weakness. Penetrating through the depth of all your wisdom and the disguises your vanity constructed, a costly pretext for your timidity! What, tyrant, do you grow pale? Your arm freezes in the air, when with a face showing no fear, I bring you my head? Take care, my executioners, not to trouble yourself. You'll miss your blow—for I make you tremble! With a blood even more hot and an arm even more firm, I will rush to hasten the end of your sunny days. With how much joy and how much strength I would thrust a dagger in your heart. In any event, if I fall short in this work I still leave a son to inherit my rage who will—to avenge the wrongs I've suffered, make your blood gush before me in Hell!"

KING

Oh—oh—why I know that—they were playing the Agrippina of Mr. Cyrano de Bergerac.

GEORGETTE

At the Théâtre Italien—it was something quite different. There was a serving girl—bright and clever, who spoke in the most comical way.

"I don't want to listen to amorous speeches—they are, in faith, evil and dangerous—I sin enough, anyway, without sinning by listening. On the subject of sinning, your empty bottle, your great faker, your dog of a valet, in the end this ill constructed, this cursed Jodelet, for the last two or three years has taken me for someone else. I would really have beaten up him but for you.

He finds me to his taste, whatever I do pleases him—but does he please me, wretch that he is? He takes me for someone of a different sort. A handsome marmoset! He's as sharp as a pike. He thinks at night he's playing guitar, so all day long I have a tortured head. In the end, he will see, if you give the order, that I scratch well enough and that I know how to bite."

KING

Bravo, Georgette!

GEORGETTE

Good! Look how the King applauds me—the way they applaud women.

KING

And that pleases you?

GEORGETTE

I should think so! Because if ever you are king—

KING

What do you mean—if ever I am King? I hope indeed that I am.

GEORGETTE

No—I mean—if ever you become it, I shall ask your patronage.

KING

You have it.

(The Master of Ceremonies, Mr. Montglat appears in the rear.)

GEORGETTE

You'll have me received as an actress in the theater?

KING

I promise you. But wait. Isn't that Molière passing by?

GEORGETTE

Yes.

KING

Well, run after him, Georgette and send him here.

GEORGETTE

Right away, Sire.

(running out)

Oh, I will be an actress! I will be an actress! The King has promised me.

KING

(turning)

Ah, it's you Mr. Master of Ceremonies.

MONTGLAT

Sire, if I'd known Your Majesty wished to speak with Mr.

Molière, I would have warned him, so that he could present himself at the King's audience with the customary ceremony.

KING

But, my dear Marquis, you know indeed that the Poquelins are upholsterers to the crown and valets de chambre to the King—father and son—under these two titles they have their grand and petty entrances.

MONTGLAT

It's true! Men of the castle. Excuse me, Sire.

KING

You've come for orders about the Cardinal's gaming tables?

MONTGLAT

I beg the King to excuse me, those orders have been received. No, I was looking for the King.

KING

You were looking for me, Marques? Well, here I am.

MONTGLAT

I wanted to ask Your Majesty if there was need for two rooms or if he desired a complete apartment.

KING

For whom?

MONTGLAT

For the new dignitary.

KING

What new dignitary, Marques?

MONTGLAT

The Secret Agent of His Majesty.

KING

Ah! Yes—but I didn't ask for rooms nor an apartment.

MONTGLAT

My duty is not only to obey the orders of the King but even to foresee his wishes.

KING

Thanks for the intention, my dear Marquis, but the person of whom you speak doesn't reside at the Château.

MONTGLAT

Ah—he doesn't reside at the castle?

KING

No.

MONTGLAT

And then if he presents himself to see the King, under what title must he be announced?

KING

He has no titles, my dear Marquis.

MONTGLAT

It remains for me to ask, Sire, if he will enter by the great doors or the corridors.

KING

He'll enter whichever way he pleases, Marquis—he has the keys to my apartment.

MONTGLAT

The keys to the King's apartment?

KING

Why, yes. You understand clearly, my dear fellow? From the moment this agent were to reside at the Château, from the moment he had a title, from the moment he was forced by you to wait to be introduced by you—he would no longer be a secret agent.

MONTGLAT

That's true. But I must tell the King what he's doing is outside all received customs—and that there is no example in court etiquette—

KING

Fine! Well, my dear Montglat, I shall set the example of etiquette instead of following it—while waiting be so obliging as to procure a passport which will open the exterior gates of the Château.

MONTGLAT

For whom?

KING

Whoever holds it—without distinction.

MONTGLAT

In an hour the King will have what he desires.

(Molière enters.)

KING

Thanks, Marquis. Now, here's Molière. I have some orders to give him—would you leave me along with him, Marquis?

MONTGLAT

I withdraw.

(low)

Doubtless Molière is charged with furnishing the apartment of the secret agent. I will follow Mr. Molière, and learn at least where this character dwells.

(leaves)

MOLIÈRE

The King does me the favor of requesting?

KING

Who says it's a favor, sir—and that I didn't call you, on the contrary to complain of you?

MOLIÈRE

That would still be a favor. But I am so sure of my love that I boldly present myself before you with the certainty that it is impossible I have offended you.

KING

Mr. Molière, it seems you are protecting Prince Condé?

MOLIÈRE

Oh, Sire, the first Prince of the blood after the Duke of Anjou, protected by a jester?

KING

You are protecting him, sir, since this very day you told Mr. Guenaud as he was leaving for Brussels that if you dared, you would tell me directly—of the Prince's desire to return to France?

MOLIÈRE

Permit me to congratulate Your Majesty on the accuracy of the reports given to him.

(saluting)

It seems his agent is in the country.

KING

Yes, sir, and despite the accuracy of his reports, I doubted for a moment his on your account.

MOLIÈRE

Why, Sire? Your Majesty asked me for a way to know the truth; I showed him one. If the King doesn't know the truth—my way was bad.

KING

Yes, but I thought that in your character as poet and actor, you were abandoning politics to those who have the misfortune to be obliged to practice it, and that you occupied yourself only with the theater.

MOLIÈRE

Well, exactly, Sire! The King knows that the Fronde is a comedy of errors—a cape and sword show, a Spanish type intrigue; in my capacity as an actor. I took a role in this comedy that's all.

KING

Yes, but luckily the comedy is reaching its denouement—look Mr. Molière, in your opinion what should the ending be? You don't recuse your competence in such matters, I presume.

MOLIÈRE

From the moment the King himself admits that the Fronde is a comedy the denouement must be a happy one.

KING

So, in your opinion, Prince Condé—

MOLIÈRE

Let the King consider that he is deigning to ask my opinion—

KING

I insist on it, Mr. Molière.

MOLIÈRE

Well, Sire, in my opinion Prince Condé should return to France without his having to request it—all the more reason since he does request to—

KING

And what will he do in France?

MOLIÈRE

What he's always done—he will win battles for Your Majesty.

KING

You're forgetting, Mr. Molière, that he's won some against me.

MOLIÈRE

Return the Prince to the place he ought to occupy beside you, Sire, and he himself will tear out from the book of his life, the page on which those fatal victories are written.

KING

Mr. Molière! Mr. Molière! You are, I know good friends with the Prince.

MOLIÈRE

Yes, Sire, but I am, at the same time, the most faithful of King Louis XIV's subjects.

KING

And what need have I of Prince Condé in France? You see things are getting on very nicely without him.

MOLIÈRE

Yes, Sire, because nations are forgetful, but when nations forget, Kings must remember. A king never passes over a great man, Sire. The Majesty of Kings is made by the greatness of those who surround them. God keep me from wishing to lower Cardinal Mazarin in your esteem—Sire, the day when he consents to initiate the King into the mysteries of his politics, the King will realize that he is not only an able minister but what we theater folk call a stage manager—he has the cleverness of a minister and the skill of a clever stage manager—but he lacks the genius of a King. So leave him the accessories, the decor, the scene changes—but reserve to yourself the intrigue of the play, the right to select the characters who must play the leading roles in the immense spectacle you are called on to give to the universe. I knew quite well that in the theater, in the days of distress—when the great actors are absent, their roles are taken by understudies; but believe me, Sire, however good they may be, a play played by understudies will never seem to the audience anything but a plain and dull parody.

KING

Mr. Molière, it's often a great mistake to raise up an enemy who is on the ground and to return arms to the disarmed.

MOLIÈRE

That's possible, Sire, but it's a sublime fault, and these faults are rare enough amongst kings so that God who observes their imprudence raising themselves to his level by their clemency, is astonished by it, but doesn't punish them!

KING

My father Louis the XIII never pardoned Mr. Molière, and his contemporaries called him Louis the Just.

MOLIÈRE

Yes, Sire, because there are periods when Providence instead of a scepter places an axe in the hands of Kings, but fortunately the days of Louis XI and Richelieu, of Constable de Saint-Pol and Marshall Montmorency are passed! What would you do today with the gibbets of Plessis les Tours or the scaffolds of Lyon and Toulouse? You are opening a new era, you are rebuilding society, with debris from the past, you are molding the world of the future—! What the father has destroyed, of necessity, the son must rebuild—that's the law—so, if one destroys with severity you have to rebuild with Clemency. Happy are those that are called by Providence to play the part of regenerators of nations, of Kings, of societies. We count one of those men in the ancient world: He's called Augustus—in the modern world; Charlemagne: In the eight centuries distance from Augustus Charlemagne came; in the eight centuries distance from Charlemagne you've come, Sire! Augustus and Charlemagne began with clemency—Louis XIV will begin like them, and God will perhaps grace him by letting him end like them.

KING

Mr. Molière—I promise you to speak of Prince Condé to my mother and Cardinal Mazarin.

MOLIÈRE

Oh! Sire! Don't submit such matters to the hate of a woman or the pusillanimity of a minister. Clemency is a royal virtue; be clement by yourself—since you are King.

KING

I am king, sir, it's true. But I hesitate for I have not yet performed a royal act.

MOLIÈRE

You'll never find a better opportunity. Begin with Clemency, Sire, and the beginning will be worthy of the grandson of Henry IV.

KING

(smiling)

It's your will—Mr. Molière?

MOLIÈRE

(paper and pen in hand, knee on the ground)

Yes, Sire—it's my will.

(Anne appears and recoils behind a door.)

KING

(writing)

"Prince Condé, return to France as soon as your health permits it, only the sooner the better for I will have great pleasure in having you by me. Yours affectionately, Louis."

Here, Molière, send this letter on my behalf and yours to Prince Condé and be at my levee tomorrow morning.

MOLIÈRE

Sire, you are still only a good King—proceed boldly on the path you've just begun and you will be a great one.

KING

(not seeing his mother)

Strange how this man has words which make you think. One would say that even in his theater, he has the ability to raise the curtain which lets you see unknown horizons and unfamiliar perspectives.

(turning)

Ah, it's you, Madame.

ANNE

Who were you with, Louis?

KING

With Molière, Madame.

ANNE

An actor, I believe! The son of Poquelin, right, who wants a license for a theater?

KING

Right.

ANNE

And you were signing his license?

KING

No, Madame, I was signing a pardon for Prince Condé.

ANNE

Pardon for Prince Condé? You are authorizing the Prince to return to France?

KING

Yes, Madame.

ANNE

Without consulting me? Without consulting Cardinal Mazarin?

KING

Pardon, Madame, but I thought the right of clemency was a royal prerogative.

ANNE

Sire, your august father never singed an act of such importance without consulting his minister.

KING

Madame, my father reigned under Mr. Richelieu, and as for me, I've decided to reign over everyone.

ANNE

Even—

(she hesitate)

KING

Over everyone, Madame!

(Marie enters resplendent with diamonds.)

ANNE

(holding the King who is going to Marie)

My son!

KING

Pardon, Madame, but here's Miss Mancini who I was waiting for here and who's counting on me to be her cavalier.

ANNE

Oh!

(The King takes Marie's hand who, fearful, looks from the King to the Queen.)

MARIE

Sire!

KING

Come, Marie! Come.

(low)

Oh! How beautiful you are—and how I love you.

(Marie, joyous and triumphant goes to her uncle's where the courtiers are beginning to arrive.)

ANNE

Three thousand crowns for Anjou! A million for Louis—! All his diamonds to his niece. Decidedly, Cardinal Mazarin thinks he's already the uncle of the—King of France. Oh, and it was I who caused the Duchess of Savoy and her daughter to be present at this shame and bear this affront.

CHARLOTTE

(entering)

Her Highness, the Regent asks Your Majesty if she can descend with Princess Marguerite to Cardinal Mazarin?

ANNE

Oh—pardon, you are?

CHARLOTTE

I am the Maid of Honor to Her Highness, Princess Marguerite.

ANNE

Yes, yes—very fine, I remember you—return to my sister-in-law and tell her—and rather—no, I'm going there myself—ah, Mazarin, you've got a score to settle with me.

CHARLOTTE

(alone)

Good! Now here's a countermand—well, if the Princesses doesn't come down, perhaps we'll have to leave without having seen the court. How amusing that is—do 200 leagues for Louis the XIV, for Cardinal Mazarin, for Henriette, for the court parties, for the hunting at Vincennes—and leave without having sampled all that! Not to mention poor Bouchavannes, who was so happy at my arrival and who found a way to tell me in a few lines—that, by special grace, he would be at the Cardinal's gaming tables tonight and we could see each other there—and decide something—oh, if he was there, if I could make a sign to him—! If I could only exchange a word with him.

(she tries to look into the next room)

BOUCHAVANNES

(entering)

Why, I'm not mistaken, it is Charlotte!

CHARLOTTE

Ah, Bouchavannes, listen, I Have only a moment to remain here, and it's a miracle that I saw you come in. The princesses are not coming down to the gaming—I received your letter—I still love you—but I'm afraid that we'll be leaving in the morning, and I know neither how nor where to return to you.

BOUCHAVANNES

Listen in your turn, Charlotte. I've explored the place. The service door to the Princesses' apartment gives on the Court of the Orangery. Throw a cloak over your shoulders and come join me—I will be on duty beneath your stairway from ten to midnight.

CHARLOTTE

Good! I will do everything I can to come down and talk with you for a moment.

GUICHE

(entering, very agitated)

Pardon, Bouchavannes.

CHARLOTTE

Here's a gentleman who wants to talk to you.

BOUCHAVANNES

Ah, it's you, Mr. de Guiche!

GUICHE

(reading a letter)

'I absolutely must speak to you tonight.'

(to Bouchavannes)

Could you let me have your duty in the Court of the Orangery?

BOUCHAVANNES

Impossible, my dear count, I have a rendezvous during my tour of duty.

(to Charlotte)

Till tonight.

CHARLOTTE

Till tonight.

(she leaves)

GUICHE

Who's on duty after you?

BOUCHAVANNES

Treville.

GUICHE

At what time?

BOUCHAVANNES

At midnight.

GUICHE

Where do you think I can find him?

BOUCHAVANNES

In the guard room.

GUICHE

Thanks!

(he leaves)

BOUCHAVANNES

Poor Guiche! My word, so much the worse! Charity begins at home—Oh—oh! The Master of Ceremonies. What an anxious look he has.

(he leaves)

MONTGLAT

(entering without seeing Bouchavannes leave and mumbling to himself)

Having been thirty years in the court, around 10,000 days, consequently having prepared 10,000 lunches, 10,000 dinners, 10,000 suppers—having seen the same faces and heard the same conversations, with the only difference that the faces get older and older and—

(Bernouin enters.)

MONTGLAT

And the conversations more and more boring—having spent fifteen years—

BERNOUIN

Pardon—Mr. Master of Ceremonies—

MONTGLAT

Ah, it's you, Bernouin! Your servant.

(back to his preoccupation)

Having been fifteen years—

BERNOUIN

Excuse me, Mr. Montglat, but would you have the goodness to tell the Cardinal—without circumlocution—that I am waiting for him here to communicate to him a matter of the highest importance?

MONTGLAT

Right away, sir.

(going into the hall at the rear)

(Guitaut enters but stops at the door in a military posture)

BERNOUIN

Ah! It's you, Mr. Guitaut!

GUITAUT

The Cardinal.

BERNOUIN

The Cardinal will be here momentarily.

GUITAUT

Can I wait for him?

BERNOUIN

Certainly. Moreover, he'll probably have some particular order for you to carry out.

HENRIETTE

(entering, and putting her arm in Guitaut's)

Dear Mr. Guitaut!

GUITAUT

Your Royal Highness!

HENRIETTE

Be so nice as to tell me the names of the Musketeers on guard tonight in the Court of the Orangery.

GUITAUT

From eight to ten this evening Mr. de Bregy; from ten to midnight Mr. de Bouchavannes; from midnight to two Mr. de Treville.

HENRIETTE

Thanks—oh, the Cardinal.

(she lets go Guitaut's arm and goes back to the party as Mazarin speaks to Bernouin)

MAZARIN

You have something to ask me, Bernouin?

BERNOUIN

Yes, Milord, to courier from the Spanish Ambassador.

MAZARIN

From Señor Pimental? Give it to me, Bernouin, let's have it.

(reading)

"Milord, I have to communicate news to you of the greatest importance which must be known only to you. Where can I see you, tonight, without witnesses and without anyone knowing I've seen you?" Egad—he mustn't enter the palace. Bernouin, a pen and paper.

BERNOUIN

Here, Milord.

MAZARIN

(after having written)

Here, Bernouin, return this response to the messenger—Egad, news from Spain—ah, it's you, Guitaut—well, King Charles—?

GUITAUT

Well, Milord, King Charles ended by listening to reason and in the morning he will leave Vincennes.

MAZARIN

Good! And Madame Henriette?

GUITAUT

What about Madame Henriette?

MAZARIN

You didn't tell her anything, Guitaut?

GUITAUT

Come on, Milord.

MAZARIN

Good Guitaut, good, you are a faithful servant and don't worry, I won't forget the 50,000 crowns for your niece.

GUITAUT

I thought it was a hundred thousand, Milord?

MAZARIN

You know the password, Guitaut?

GUITAUT

Yes, but not the countersign.

MAZARIN

The countersign is to let in anyone who comes to the small gate of the Orangery, and raps thrice saying, "France and Spain."

GUITAUT

That suffices, Milord.

MAZARIN

News from Spain—ah—Mercy!

(he leaves)

BERNOUIN

The Devil! I believe His Eminence is in a bad mood.

GUITAUT

Yes, and his bad mood makes him lose his memory. Still, if he can recall those 50,000 crowns, that's all I ask of him.

(Bernouin and Guitaut leave by different sides.)

MONTGLAT

(entering the preceding, still grumbling)

After fifteen years as a grand master of ceremonies, that is to say having exercised this important duty for five thousand days and five thousand nights, having constantly known who entered to the King's presence and who left—there comes a time when an unknown man leaves and enters without my knowing when or how! Now this is one of those humiliations reserved by new regimes for old servants! This is one of those acts of distrust which drive a grand master of ceremonies to despair.

(Villequier and Dangeau enter and approach Montglat on either side.)

MONTGLAT

Still, this cannot last, in my view at least, and at the first opportunity, I shall stand before the King and say to him with all the respect I owe him, and the dignity I retain for myself—

VILLEQUIER

Look, who are you talking to, Montglat?

MONTGLAT

Ah, it's you, Villequier!

DANGEAU

We are listening.

MONTGLAT

Ah, it's you, Dangeau! Well, I will say to him, "Sire, Your Majesty has taken a step which saddens the hearts of his faithful subjects! Sire, Your Majesty scrupulously preserves the incognito of your secret agent, but despite Your Majesty's silence, this agent has been seen, this man is known, and something about his past leaks out, which worries the friends of the King over the future! They are all saying darkly that the weight of this unknown hand is becoming unbearable, they say—

KING

(entering)

Montglat.

VILLEQUIER and DANGEAU

The King.

(They separate one to the left and one to the right.)

MONTGLAT

Sire?

KING

(low)

Have you the key I asked you for?

MONTGLAT

Here it is, Sire.

KING

Thanks.

(he pulls a letter from his pocket and reads it)

"Be in the Orangery tonight, a secret of importance will be revealed to you there." Who could have written me that? Never mind, I'll be there.

(he moves away)

VILLEQUIER

(going to Dangeau)

Well?

DANGEAU

The King was speaking low.

VILLEQUIER

What did he say to you?

MONTGLAT

Gentleman, the King did me the honor of confiding to me the name of this mysterious unknown.

VILLEQUIER

And this name?

DANGEAU

What name?

MONTGLAT

(proudly)

The King confided the secret to me, gentlemen—do like me— try to learn it.

CURTAIN

ACT IV

The Court of the Orangery. Starry skies.

In the front to the right, an archway leading to the Château. Further back a turret pierced by a window and a door giving on an interior staircase. The back is closed by a wall over which the foliage of trees extend. In this wall, a small, usable gate. To the left, towards the back part of a building adjoining the Orangery; Window on a balcony which can be reached by standing on a bench placed beneath it. In the angle, the Orangery with large windows three feet off the ground, a terrace surrounding it. Close to the audience on the left side a passage entering the Orangery whose door cannot be seen.

Bouchavannes and two other musketeers come to relieve Bregy, the guard on duty.

BOUCHAVANNES

The password?

BREGY

Fortune and Fontainbleau.

BOUCHAVANNES

The countersign.

BREGY

Allow in any person who raps thrice at the small exterior gate and says Spain and France.

BOUCHAVANNES

Thanks.

BREGY

Have fun, Bouchavannes!

BOUCHAVANNES

Well, I don't say no. I really love night patrols.

(Bregy goes off with the two other Musketeers to the left through the passageway which runs along the Orangery.)

BOUCHAVANNES

Ten o'clock—that's fine; patience—I mustn't expect Charlotte until an hour from now. Let's see—let's get acclimated. Here's the stairway leading to the Princesses' chamber—and by which Charlotte will come—if Charlotte comes—; there's the little gate where the person who must be let in must knock; there's the window of Miss Mancini's room—that lodging, is, on my oath, well chosen, isolated, solitary—you can see that the King's love has played quartermaster of the camp and prepared his billet— finally, here's the Orangery—

(returning to his post)

Oh! Oh! Someone—a woman! Can it be Charlotte already? Why no, she wouldn't come this way. Who goes there?

HENRIETTE

You are Mr. de Bouchavannes?

BOUCHAVANNES

Yes. What do wish?

HENRIETTE

Look at me, sir.

BOUCHAVANNES

The Princess Henriette.

HENRIETTE

Who's come in the name of her mother and herself to ask a favor of you, sir—

BOUCHAVANNES

Rather to give me an order, Your Highness means.

HENRIETTE

Alas, no, Mr. de Bouchavannes—you know quite well that we have no orders to give him, and that on the contrary, it is we who receive them, and very hard ones sometimes.

BOUCHAVANNES

But, My God, what can bring Your Highness at this hour to this solitary court?

HENRIETTE

I was looking for you, sir.

BOUCHAVANNES

Me?

HENRIETTE

You are a gentleman, sir, you have a mother, a sister—you know the emotions of a family—sometimes sweet, sometimes and— well, if you were separated from your sister for three years— and your sister was wandering, proscribed, a fugitive you would feel a compelling need, to see her again and you wouldn't hesitate to confide this desire to a friend—Mr. Bouchavannes you are a friend to us, it was my mother, if I am not mistaken who put you near the Princess of Savoy.

BOUCHAVANNES

And you know, Madame, that the gratitude of my family is assured to your august mother and to you.

HENRIETTE

Oh! Let's not speak anymore of gratitude, that would give a limit to your devotion and I prefer to make an appeal to it— completely, absolutely, entirely.

BOUCHAVANNES

Speak, Madame, I will be happy the day when you give me the opportunity to run some danger for you.

HENRIETTE

I spoke to you of a sister, proscribed fugitive exiled. Well, as for me, sir, I have a brother, exiled, fugitive proscribed—a brother that I haven't seen for three years.

BOUCHAVANNES

King Charles II?

HENRIETTE

King Charles the Second, yes, sir. Well, King Charles the Second is here at Vincennes, on the other side of that gate—kicked out of France today by Cardinal Mazarin, tomorrow at daybreak he leaves, he returns to Holland, Mr. Bouchavannes, I would really like to see him again, I would really like to embrace my brother, I would really like to say goodbye to him.

BOUCHAVANNES

And that's all you had to ask of me, Madame?

HENRIETTE

Yes.

BOUCHAVANNES

Were my head at stake to promise you that joy, I would risk my head—I risk a few days of arrest, a month of prison perhaps—

truly, Madame, I am ashamed to do so little for you.

(going to the small gate and opening it)

Enter, sir—Madam Henriette is waiting for you.

CHARLES

Sister!

HENRIETTE

Brother!

(Charles offers his hand amicably to Bouchavannes.)

BOUCHAVANNES

(Kissing the King's hand and withdrawing)

Sire, I am watching over you and your sister.

CHARLES

Oh, my good little Henriette! Poor guardian angel of the family—how much I thank you for what you are doing for me. Where is our mother? How is she?

HENRIETTE

Mother's waiting for you—she's going to be very happy to see you again. Come! Come! Oh, Mr. Bouchavannes receive all the gratitude of a mother and sister.

BOUCHAVANNES

Go! But don't forget think that I have only an hour and a half of duty, and that if I were replaced before he could proceed to go back through this court—

GEORGETTE

(on the terrace of the Orangery)

Sire!

BOUCHAVANNES

Silence! It seems to me someone's talking in whispers.

HENRIETTE

Oh—watch over us, Mr. Bouchavannes!

BOUCHAVANNES

Don't worry—I won't leave this arch—and no one will pass unless they have the pass word.

HENRIETTE

Come Charles, come!

GEORGETTE

(still on the terrace)

Sire! Oh, my God—he doesn't hear me—and I cannot come down! Sire—

(she breaks a branch off a tree and with it strikes the window above her. The King opens the window)

KING

Is it you, Georgette?

GEORGETTE

It's me, Sire—hush, there's a guard down there.

KING

I've seen him indeed. That imbecile Guitaut—putting a guard right under the window of Miss Mancini.

GEORGETTE

It's true—who could imagine that? But there indeed are other things, Sire!

KING

What's wrong?

GEORGETTE

My father has just received the order to hold this Orangery ready for Cardinal Mazarin—I hid the key so he couldn't get in, but the Cardinal has a second key.

KING

And your father—where is he?

GEORGETTE

He went to find the Cardinal with his lantern.

KING

But what the devil is Mazarin coming to do here, at this hour in the Orangery?

GEORGETTE

Ah, as to that I don't know, but it seems he gave a rendezvous to someone. Ms. Bernouin himself came to get the key.

KING

Why didn't you tell me that when you introduced me into the Orangery?

GEORGETTE

I didn't know it yet—hush!

KING

What?

GEORGETTE

Someone's coming.

KING

Yes, two men, one carrying a lantern.

BOUCHAVANNES

Who goes?

MAN WITH A LANTERN

Fortune and Fontainbleau.

BOUCHAVANNES

Pass.

MAZARIN

You know the countersign, Bouchavannes?

BOUCHAVANNES

Your Eminence!

MAZARIN

You know it?

BOUCHAVANNES

Yes, Milord, let anyone enter who—

MAZARIN

Right. Good show, Mr. Bouchavannes. Good show.

(The Man with the Lantern and Mazarin pass before the window of the Orangery which closes as they pass and reopens behind them.)

KING

It's indeed the Cardinal? What to do? If I try to leave, I'm going to meet him at the door!

BOUCHAVANNES

(to himself)

At least King Charles didn't meet him.

GEORGETTE

Sire, sire, be careful.

KING

Eh, by God! I hear him quite well! He's putting the key in the lock—he's going to enter—ah, my word, so much the worse. No one can see me. The Royal Majesty is saved.

(he climbs over the balcony)

GEORGETTE

Sire, sire, the guard!

KING

Oh, what an idea!

BOUCHAVANNES

(barring the way with his musket)

Who goes?

KING

Mr. de Bouchavannes!

BOUCHAVANNES

Who goes?

KING

I am the King, sir—your hat, your cloak, your musket, I will finish your watch.

BOUCHAVANNES

Oh—Sire—

KING

The password?

BOUCHAVANNES

Fortune and Fontainbleau.

KING

The countersign?

BOUCHAVANNES

To let in whoever knocks three times at the little wooden gate—who says France and Spain.

KING

Who's on guard after you?

BOUCHAVANNES

Mr. de Treville.

KING

Fine, sir, return to your room and come to my chamber tomorrow to receive your captain's commission.

BOUCHAVANNES

Sire!

KING

Go!

(they close the window from the Orangery)

Get going then!

BOUCHAVANNES

Oh, poor Charlotte—and Madame Henriette and King Charles—Ah, my word—God protect them!

(goes off)

(A voice can be heard calling "Georgette.")

GEORGETTE

You don't need me anymore, Sire?

KING

No.

GEORGETTE

It's my father calling me.

VOICE

Georgette.

KING

Go.

(She disappears.)

KING

(alone)

It seems to me Mr. de Bouchavannes, resisted strangely, giving me the countersign and surrendering to me his musket. Did he have some interest in staying on his watch? We're going to find out—but it's Cardinal Mazarin who worries me. What kind of affair can he leave in the Orangery at this hour and who can he be expecting? It's not to spy on his niece since he shut the window from the Orangery and lowered the blinds. No matter, this is going to make it very difficult to let Marie know I am here.

CHARLOTTE

(at the turret window)

Mr. de Bouchavannes.

KING

(turning)

Huh?

CHARLOTTE

You are there, aren't you?

KING

Yes, but—

CHARLOTTE

It's me, Charlotte, the princesses are in bed, they are sleeping and I am here.

KING

(aside)

Oh, the maid of honor to the Regent. I understand; Bouchavannes' mother is near Madame Christine and he spent three months at the Court of Savoy.

CHARLOTTE

Well—can I come down?

KING

Indeed.

CHARLOTTE

Then you are alone?

KING

Completely alone.

CHARLOTTE

I am coming down.

KING

Good, I am going to have fresh news from Turin.

CHARLOTTE

(on stage)

Here I am.

KING

Come here in the shadow, Charlotte, so that no one can see us.

CHARLOTTE

Oh, how happy I am to be able to talk freely with you for a moment.

KING

Me, too.

CHARLOTTE

(giving him her hand to keep)

Here.

KING

(aside)

Well, night duty's not so disagreeable and I thought till now.

CHARLOTTE

Imagine how afraid I was that I'd be obliged to leave again without being able to speak to you.

KING

And why's that?

CHARLOTTE

Why because you've heard we are not going to remain at Vincennes, right?

KING

I don't understand.

CHARLOTTE

What—you don't understand? Why you must realize we've made a pointless trip?

KING

Ah, yes—the King.

CHARLOTTE

The King is mad for Miss Mancini that's all! You know it's seriously a question of marriage?

KING

Bah?

CHARLOTTE

Oh—the Queen Mother is furious—she said that if she had only the King to manage, she could do it; but it's this trickster of a Mazarin who's behind the intrigue. The Regent Christine spent the whole evening in tears. Hell, it's quite natural—she already thought her daughter was Queen of France.

KING

And Princess Marguerite?

CHARLOTTE

Oh—she made a pretense of being very sad.

KING

What do you mean a pretense?

CHARLOTTE

Yes, but—

KING

But?

CHARLOTTE

But deep down, I think she's quite happy.

KING

Really? Oh—explain that to me. Princess Marguerite is happy that the King is marrying Miss Mancini?

CHARLOTTE

Oh! My God—Miss Mancini or someone else, as long as he doesn't marry her.

KING

She detests the King?

CHARLOTTE

No—but she loves someone else.

KING

Bah?

CHARLOTTE

Yes—the Queen's invitation fell like a bomb in the midst of these lovers. Ah, there were tears—almost as many as when we parted, dear Hector.

(she presents her face to be kissed)

KING

(aside, embracing her)

Now I understand why Bouchavannes was reluctant to give up his watch to me.

CHARLOTTE

Huh?

KING

But who does she love then?

CHARLOTTE

My princess?

KING

Yes.

CHARLOTTE

She loves Don Ranuce, Prince Farnese, Duke of Parma and Plaisanu, my father is his great squire, as you know.

KING

No, I don't know.

CHARLOTTE

Oh, a handsome young man of twenty-eight almost as handsome as the King.

KING

And you say she prefers to be Duchess of Parma to being Queen of France? At least she's not ambitious.

CHARLOTTE

Hell, it's quite natural: She loves Prince Farnese and doesn't love King Louis. Isn't it the same as me loving you? Wouldn't I prefer to be the Viscomtess de Bouchavannes to being the Duchess of Parma? For heaven's sake!

KING

Really?

CHARLOTTE

Ah, you doubt it? That's nice, after—

KING

After what?

CHARLOTTE

Hush!

KING

But still, if the King had married Princess Marguerite, Prince Farnese—

CHARLOTTE

Oh! The prince had quite decided to follow her to the court of France, even if he had to renounce his principality.

KING

Good! Happily Prince Farnese won't have to inconvenience himself.

CHARLOTTE

Yes, happily.

KING

Ah, yes! But you have an interest in the marriage of the Duke of Parma with the Princess of Savoy?

CHARLOTTE

A very great one! If Princess Marguerite marries the Duke, our marriage will take place.

KING

How's that?

CHARLOTTE

The day of her marriage, the Duke of Farnese will give me one hundred thousand pounds as a wedding gift—so that—if on your side, you have only a company—

KING

I have it.

CHARLOTTE

What do you mean, you have it?

KING

The King promised it to me this evening—it's as if I had it.

CHARLOTTE

Good—And Cardinal Mazarin's permission—does the King have that? A company is worth 40,000 pounds.

KING

And as for me, I tell you it's as if I had it, Charlotte.

CHARLOTTE

Oh! What luck! What luck!

(jumps on his neck and kisses him)

KING

(aside)

Ah, indeed, much better to be Bouchavannes than the King—it seem to me.

CHARLOTTE

Hush!

KING

What?

CHARLOTTE

Two people are coming that way.

KING

Yes—indeed. Go back in, Charlotte, go back in.

CHARLOTTE

So, you think the King will marry Miss Mancini?

KING

Eh! Eh! It's probable.

CHARLOTTE

Anyway, you think so?

KING

It's possible, but in any case, he won't marry Princess Marguerite.

CHARLOTTE

No?

KING

Oh, no.

CHARLOTTE

Then the Princess will marry Duke Farnese?

KING

I'll do what I can about that.

CHARLOTTE

You still love me?

KING

Hush, they're coming.

(pushing her in the turret stairway)

KING

(barring their way)

Who goes there?

HENRIETTE

(coming forward)

Don't you recognize us, Mr. Bouchavannes?

KING

Yes! Yes!

(aside)

Henriette, my cousin. And who's she got with her ?

CHARLES

Mr. de Bouchavannes, I thank you for it's to you I owe one of the pleasantest hours I've spent in a long time.

KING

Charles II! Charles II in France, in Paris, in Vincennes.

CHARLES

I've given Cardinal Mazarin my word not to see either King Louis or the Queen Mother, but I didn't promise him not to see my mother or my sister. I've had the joy of seeing both of them again and it's to you that I owe it.

HENRIETTE

And believe this, dear Mr. Bouchavannes, if they ever learn that you have done for us, if they want to punish your compassion for poor exiles, I am going to throw myself at the feet of my cousin, Louis, who is so good that nothing bad will happen to you.

KING

Thanks.

(aside)

Darling Henriette.

CHARLES

Au revoir, dear sir—and God protect you—come, dear little sister, so I won't have to leave you until the very last moment. Alas! I indeed regret not having seen the King.

(Charles and Henriette go the back, the King keeps close enough to them so he can hear what they are saying.)

KING

(aside)

He regrets not having seen me!

HENRIETTE

Explain to me anyway what you wanted to ask him and perhaps the opportunity will present itself.

CHARLES

Listen carefully to this, little sister, although this must seem grave and very serious for you—

HENRIETTE

I don't know if one day I'll become happy and gay again, but I do know, that up to now misfortune has made me serious and grave enough to accomplish whatever you can tell me.

CHARLES

Well, now that Cromwell is dead, there's a man who holds the destiny of England in his hands—he has only to say a word to overthrow Richard, Cromwell's son, and to raise me to the throne. That man is in Scotland, he has an army and if I had a million, perhaps I would have that man.

HENRIETTE

A million! Oh, my God—Mazarin, who has so many millions—and what's this man's name?

CHARLES

His name is Monk. Although the thing may be unlikely, perhaps my cousin, Louis, could lend me that million, and then poor exiles that we are, there would be a chance of our fortunes, changing—and we would become ourselves again: Me, a real king and you, a true Princess Royal.

HENRIETTE

And perhaps then too, my cousin Louis, who I love so much and who doesn't even look at me, would pay attention to poor little Henriette—ah!

KING

(aside)

Heavens! Ah, darling cousin—and I never suspected any of this!

CHARLES

Go, we must leave each other—ah, tomorrow exile will begin again; exile that I, for an instant, felt was over tonight. Adieu, sister!

HENRIETTE

Goodbye, Charles, goodbye.

CHARLES

Let me hug you one more time, one for you and one for mother— Ah, if ever I become King again, how I'll try to make her forget what she suffered.

HENRIETTE

And as for me, I am going to try to make her wait until you are King less sad—Adieu!

CHARLES

Adieu!

(He leaves, Henriette shuts the gate after him.)

HENRIETTE

Oh, Mr. Bouchavannes, be sure I will never forget what you've just done for us.

(she leaves)

KING

Poor Charles! Poor Henriette! Ah, its' a sad and grim world that of politics, especially when it's done the way Mazarin does it. So each has his sum of desires in this world—Georgette wants to be an actress—Molière wants a license; Bouchavannes solicits a company—Charlotte asks for one hundred thousand pounds, Charles needs a million, Henriette—poor little Henriette— she's the only one perhaps who won't have what she desires— Ah, Mr. Bouchavannes, my word, for the service you've done me, it's not a company I owe you, it's a regiment.

(noticing Charlotte at the window)

What are you there?

CHARLOTTE

I told you that I still love you, I am waiting for you to tell me that you still love me.

KING

(aside)

There's no escaping it.

(aloud)

More than ever.

CHARLOTTE

And if you get your company, you will marry me?

KING

Yes.

CHARLOTTE

Even if I don't have my one hundred thousand pounds?

KING

Even if you don't have them.

CHARLOTTE

Ohhh, how sweet you are! Oh how I love you—Till tomorrow.

KING

Till tomorrow.

(aside)

Ah, my word, so much the worse. Mr. de Bouchavannes, there you are—married.

(Charlotte disappears)

(Midnight strikes)

KING

Midnight already. A watch never seemed shorter to me. Ah, indeed, but I haven't even had time to let Marie know that I am here. Good—someone is coming to relieve me.

GUICHE

(as a musketeer with two others)

The password.

KING

Fortune and Fontainbleau.

GUICHE

The countersign?

KING

Let anyone enter who—ah, indeed but when did you join the Musketeers, Guiche?

GUICHE

The King.

KING

Go to your quarter and stay under arrest until a new order, sir—I will pull your duty as I have done that of Mr. Bouchavannes.

GUICHE

But, Sire!

KING

Go to your quarters and not a word—you either, gentlemen, you hear?

ALL

(bowing)

Sire!

(they leave)

KING

(alone)

Guiche disguised as a musketeer! What did Guiche come here to do in that disguise? Tonight, I saw him approach Marie twice, twice he spoke to her, once it occured to me that their hands touched, and still, I'd stifled all suspicion, and God knows that coming here I had no intention of spying on him. Here I am and in the disguise the Count took as well—until now, you would say truly, that the hand of Providence has ordered events tonight. Let's see it through to the end even if I learn something that may be reserved to sadden me. Perhaps there may be a supreme lesson in what I remain to learn—perhaps I was about to commit some great mistake which God wishes to spare me—it seems to me there's the noise of a window opening—no—yes—it's Marie's window—let's see, and let's not forget that from the moment he replaced Mr. de Treville—it's the Count de Guiche who's standing guard from midnight until 2:00 in the morning.

MARIE

Are you there, Count?

KING

(aside)

Oh! So she really was expecting him!

MARIE

Armand.

(the King goes closer)

It's really you, right?

KING

Ah—why since everyone here is deceiving me, let's fight with the same weapons.

(to Marie)

Yes, it's me.

MAZARIN

Mr. de Treville consented to give you his watch?

KING

And you, Marie, have you agreed to grant me that favor I've begged you for so earnestly?

MARIE

Yes, Armand, for I thought an explanation was absolutely necessary between us and that I must no longer deceive you with the King or deceive the King with you—since the King is occupying himself with me, Count, and particularly yesterday at the Louvre and today at the Hunt, tonight at the Cardinal's, you've made me shiver twenty times with your jealousy.

KING

Why indeed, haven't I some reason to be jealous, Marie?

MARIE

Yes, but the more reasons you have to be jealous, Armand, the less you should show it. If you really loved me, if you loved my happiness, if you loved my future.. I granted you this rendez-vous because I don't want, I cannot allow this intrigue to go any further. So give me back my word for in the situation we are in a gentleman must do so, or tell me bluntly, "I have your word, Marie, you've said you loved me, you've written it, I demand that you sacrifice the King's love to it, and whatever future that love may promise you!" If it was today, a question of simply being the mistress of King Louis XIV, I think you ought not to hesitate and I would have no right to the sacrifice I am demanding of you—but the King is serious about me—he loves me to the point of making me his wife. I don't have his word yet, but he's ready to give it to me—and if he gives it to me, He will keep it. You know what my uncle says, "there's enough material in the King to make four honest men." Armand, do you want to snatch the crown of France from the face where you said you wanted to put the world's crown?

KING

Why then, Marie, you love the King?

MARIE

Listen to me, Armand, and believe that the high position which I am near attaining remains apart from what I am going to say to you. I am not speaking to you here of the son of Louis XIII, of the grandson of Henry the IV, of he who commands twenty-five million men. I am speaking to you about a handsome, noble and seductive gentleman who were he a simple count, or a simple baron, would still have within him, in his youth, in his grace, and in his charm, all the advantages which can seduce a woman. It wasn't surprising that my heart inclined toward you at first, hesitates now between the King and you—but to what I've just told you add this: The King is King—and I repeat he's almost engaged to marry me. Armand, don't make me repent all my life the feeling you've inspired in me. You know better than anyone that small steps we've taken on the road to this love—I've granted you nothing more than innocent favors, or fleeting promises—Armand, return my letters to me, here, as I return you yours—leave the court under the first pretext that comes along—cease to excite the jealousy of the King—remember his break up with Miss de la Motte when it was proved that she loved Charmante. Let me fulfill this marvelous destiny, allow me to follow that fortune which leads me so far from the fortune of my sisters, so many times envied by me—and I will bless you, Armand, and even more, I will love you like my true, like my best friend!

KING

Thanks, Marie, you promised me to be frank and my good fortune wills that you have been. I came here full of joy and hope—Marie, you've just broken my happiness, by blowing out that first youthful flame that the same woman always lights and extinguishes. Marie, don't be angry with me for my promptness in obeying you. I am like the King—I don't want to share love—what I need is a double virginity of heart and soul. Marie, Marie, I tell you with my eyes full of tears, this moment, you are free! I leave you.

MARIE

Armand!

KING

Goodbye, Marie. Tomorrow you will have your letters and the one whose presence you fear—the one whose love dared to enter in combat with the love of a king, the one whose jealousy you need not fear threatening you—that one will leave the court.

(three knocks at the gate.)

MARIE

(tries to take his hand.)

Armand!

KING

(rejecting her hand)

A man that your uncle is expecting in the Orangery is knocking at the gate, Marie. I am on guard and my instructions are to open for him. Return to your room and lock your window so no one besides me will see you or hear you.

MARIE

And tomorrow I will have my letters.

KING

You will have them—word of a gentleman.

MARIE

Thanks.

(she locks the window)

KING

(alone)

Oh my God, my God! Is it for my happiness or is it for my despair, you've torn the veil from my eyes?

But they're knocking for the second time—yes, yes, I hear and I'm coming.

(at the gate)

You are the person Cardinal Mazarin is expecting?

PIMENTEL

Yes.

KING

You have the password then?

PIMENTEL

Spain and France.

KING

And you bring news from Madrid?

PIMENTEL

The most important.

KING

The Queen of Spain has given birth.

PIMENTEL

Yes.

KING

Boy or a girl?

PIMENTEL

But, sir, this secret should only be confided to the Cardinal.

KING

Oh—I hope all the same, that you will be so good as to tell me before telling him?

PIMENTEL

And who are you to speak in this tone to the ambassador of Spain?

KING

I am the King of France, sir.

PIMENTEL

Oh, many excuses, Sire! But how to recognize you in this disguise?

KING

I had an order to give to the Captain of the Guards who's making his rounds tonight. Go wait for me under that archway, sir, and we'll continue this conversation in my apartment.

(Pimentel bows and goes to the archway.)

(Guitaut and four guardsmen appear.)

KING

Come here, Mr. Guitaut.

(raising his hat)

You recognize me?

(a musketeer lights the King's face with a lantern)

GUITAUT

The King—Your Majesty has some order to give me?

KING

You will arrest the Count de Guiche instantly—here I am, Mr. Pimentel.

(he disappears with the Spanish ambassador)

GUITAUT

Ah—the King is really King at last!

SERGEANT

Why's that, Captain?

GUITAUT

He just ordered me to arrest the Count de Guiche.

CURTAIN

ACT V

The King's apartment.

Several courtiers including Montglat, Dangeau, and Villequier await the rising of the King.

MONTGLAT

(pulling out his watch)

8:05: gentlemen, the King is five minutes late for the hour of his rising! His Majesty must be indisposed.

VILLEQUIER

Or, what is even more likely, His Majesty may be with his secret agent.

DANGEAU

That wouldn't surprise me! I saw a man enter the Château this morning whose face is completely unknown to me.

VILLEQUIER

What age?

DANGEAU

Thirty-four to thirty-six, black eyes, sad face, mustaches.

VILLEQUIER

You know who he is, Montglat?

MONTGLAT

Who?

VILLEQUIER

The secret agent does. His description corresponds to that given
by Dangeau?

MONTGLAT

Yes, and no, gentlemen, His Majesty's secret agent, so as not to
be recognized, changes his age three or four times; his appearance and his dress by day and twice as often by night.

DANGEAU

Why, doesn't he ever sleep?

MONTGLAT

(seriously)

Very little ! This faculty joined with hyper activity allows this
extraordinary man to fulfill , with as much exactitude as perse-
verance, the tiresome job he's undertaken.

VILLEQUIER

Then, you think Montglat that he is with the King?

MONTGLAT

I don't affirm that, but as yesterday evening the King asked me for a key to the outer gates of the Château, I only conjecture that this morning he has a lot of news and secrets to tell us.

DANGEAU

Speaking of news, gentlemen, you know that the two ladies who arrived yesterday at Vincennes incognito are none other than the Duchess of Savoy and her daughter, Princess Marguerite.

MONTGLAT

It was I who sent them their carriages from Orleans.

VILLEQUIER

As to secrets, you know that Senor Pimentel, the Spanish Ambassador left the King's apartment at two this morning?

MONTGLAT

It was I who awaited him at the gate and introduced him to the King's bedchamber.

DANGEAU

Gentlemen, all that is less astonishing than the arrest of Mr. de Guiche effected at four o'clock by Guitaut.

VILLEQUIER

Impossible! Guiche, the King's favorite?

MONTGLAT

As for this news, I give it to you as certain. It was I who awakened Guitaut—the good fellow was in a deep sleep!

DANGEAU

All this explains why His Majesty is ten minutes late, gentlemen.

MONTGLAT

(looking at his watch)

Eleven and a half—also, I repeat, doubtless something serious is happening.

MOLIÈRE

(entering)

Gentlemen, His Majesty begs you to receive his regrets, he won't have the petit levee this morning—he desires nonetheless that no one go away, having, he says, an important communication for the court.

VILLEQUIER

Who's this?

DANGEAU

The very man I saw enter Vincennes this morning.

VILLEQUIER

The secret agent?

MONTGLAT

Eh, no gentlemen—he's the new valet de chambre to His Majesty. Mr. Molière is the son of old Poquelin, upholsterer to the crown; he's an actor that the King has taken a liking to, I don't know why. I do know this because Bontemps, the valet de chambre, yesterday refused to make His Majesty's bed with the newcomer, under the pretext that he didn't associate with mountebanks. I can answer to you for that. Bontemps came to consult me about it because of my exhaustive knowledge of etiquette.

DANGEAU

And you held Bontemps right or wrong?

MONTGLAT

I held him wrong—there's an edict of Louis XIII, dated 16 April 1641, forbidding that blame be imputed to the acting profession.

MOLIÈRE

You've understood, gentlemen.

MONTGLAT

Tell the King, Mr. Molière, that we remain at his disposal according to his order.

(The courtiers file out.)

MOLIÈRE

(alone)

Well, it seems the advice I gave His Majesty had its effect. Here it is no longer a question of the King having a secret agent—everyone has seen him—one, coming on horseback, another going by foot—this one—walking sadly and thoughtfully in the most solitary paths of the pack—this one gaily tossing biscuits to swans in the great pool—he's dark, he's blond, he's brown, he's tall, he's short! Montglat had a rendezvous with him tonight. Villequier is lunching with him tomorrow morning. Dangeau hesitates to receive him, because being certain of his lineage and that he can ride in the carriages of the King—meanwhile, each decreases the hopes and plans of his neighbor—and even confesses his own—for fear of being discovered by the secret agent. The King is receiving letter after letter, confidence upon confidence—oh, pour playthings of ambition of power and fortune, who pompously take the title of men—as indeed you really are—groveling on the surface of the earth, be it in the times of Aristophanes, be it in the time of Plautus and I was going to say proud thing that I am, be it in mine—!

KING

(entering with Guitaut and looking at a stack of letters)

Thanks, Guitaut. And what did he say when you arrested him?

GUITAUT

What they all say when they are arrested, "I don't know why His Majesty—" But when I asked him for the letters of the person who sent him his back, he seemed to understand and gave me this packet without difficulty.

KING

That's fine, Guitaut. Return to Mr. de Guiche and tell him he is free—but on the condition that he rejoin the army and that he not return to Paris until I recall him.

GUITAUT

Your Majesty's orders will be punctually accomplished.

(he bows and leaves)

KING

I am free, it seems, Molière?

MOLIÈRE

Yes, Sire—but as the King desires no one has left.

KING

That's fine, sir—here's the list of persons that I intend to receive this morning. Thanks to the advice you gave me twenty-four hours ago, things have happened so rapidly that the comedy in which I've given you the role of my advisor has reached its final act—you saw the beginning, Molière, you shall see the end.

MOLIÈRE

Sire, it is impossible to be more grateful to the King one respects, to the sovereign one adores, than I am to Your Majesty; still it is impossible to be more profoundly touched than I am by the bounties with which the grandson of Henry IV honors a poor poet. But dare I say to Your Majesty that once this comedy is finished, I ask his permission to withdraw and to return to my life in the theater? I am not a man of the court—I am a poor bohemian like Callot or Salvator Rosa, holding a paint-brush in one hand, a pen in the other, doodling, scribbling, King amongst my equals. I am a slave here—honored in the wings of my theater to the equal of an emperor—I am scorned in the antechamber of the King like a pariah. For example, if the King slept ill last night, this insomnia will be attributed to the way in which his bed was made.

KING

Yes, I know that Molière: Bontemps refused to make my bed with you under the pretext, doubtless, not that a poet was not his equal, but that he was not the equal of a poet—that what you took for pride was actually humility. All the same this debt my old Bontemps has vis-a-vias you, I take as my own, Molière, and we will settle it today, together. Meanwhile take a look at my list—and see to it no one is introduced to me who is not on it.

MOLIÈRE

If I dared to observe to Your Majesty a name is missing?

KING

Whose, sir?

MOLIÈRE

It's that of my father, isn't he to come this morning for a certain letter de cachet whose end is to have imprisoned that bad actor son of his?

KING

You are right. Give the order for him to enter if he presents himself.

(Molière leaves.)

KING

(falling into an armchair)

Oh! Louis! Louis! You wanted to be King and you cannot even be a man! How do you bear, poor neophyte of power the weight of empire—you who don't know how to bear the weight of sorrow? Here are her letters—the letters Marie sent to someone other than me. I haven't read them; I won't read them—but without doubt, what she wrote to me, before writing me, she wrote to him! Aside from changing names and titles perhaps—who knows—the same letter would serve both of us! For certain, at least she said, she said it again—to each of us—those three sweet and terrible words—that perpetual lie with which woman cradle us from birth to our tomb 'I love you'.

(sadly)

Oh, me too, I loved you, Marie! I loved you to the point of madness—enough to make you my wife, to make you a queen! If someone had come to tell me what I heard last night—I wouldn't have wanted to believe it—you yourself disabused me! Thanks, Marie for that cruel cure of the sweet wound you caused me—someone's coming—Henriette—another bleeding heart. This one, at least, I can cure.

HENRIETTE

(entering)

Sire!

KING

Come here, dear Henriette, and look at me.

HENRIETTE

Oh, My God, Sire, do you know that if your look was not so kind, and your voice so affectionate, I would be very fearful.

KING

And why's that?

HENRIETTE

You wanted to see me this morning, to see me alone, to speak to me privately—what could you have to say to a poor child like me?

KING

(looking at her with great tenderness)

I have to tell you, Henriette, that you not only have beautiful eyes, a charming mouth, a admirable hair—but also a noble heart.

HENRIETTE

Cousin!

KING

You've always been a good and tender daughter consoling your mother in her sorrow—today you are a faithful and devoted sister, consoling your brother in exile.

HENRIETTE

My God! What do you mean?

KING

That I find it beautiful and grand, my dear Henriette, that when a brother is dethroned, proscribed, fugitive, when an unjust and tyrannical command forces him to leave the country which ought to be his second home—to comfort him, at least with caresses and tears—alas, poor child, that's all you were able to give him—to soften at least the cruel hour of departure.

HENRIETTE

Oh, my God! My God! Your secret agent has told you all this—

(falling to her knees)

Pardon, Sire, pardon—

KING

Not only do I pardon you, but again I congratulate you, Henriette. Now listen.

HENRIETTE

Oh, yes, I am listening, but it seems to me I'm dreaming.

KING

I am going to prove that you are awake, darling cousin. Last night, as he left you, your brother told you—near the little gate to the Orangery—you remember? That a million would probably be all he required to buy Mr. Monk?

HENRIETTE

My God! My God!

KING

Here, in this purse, is the million that your brother wanted—take it to him, Henriette. I want him to take it from your hand—if the negotiations succeed, well, it is to you and to you alone that He will owe the throne of England.

HENRIETTE

But this million—Sire—

(with sadness)

It was sent me by Cardinal Mazarin for the parties I was to give, but heart in mourning—and you must know this, Henriette—a heart in mourning flees noise, pleasures; I don't need this million—Henriette; I give it to you without regret—take it without remorse. May your brother only pardon me for doing so little now, perhaps later I will do more—much more—

HENRIETTE

Oh, thanks! Thanks!

KING

Go, dear Henriette, don't waste time—Your brother must leave this morning. I hope he has not yet left.

HENRIETTE

Oh—will you allow me to go myself?

KING

I want that.

(escorting her to the door)

HENRIETTE

How good you are!

(she starts to leave)

D'ANJOU

(in the antechamber)

Louis, Louis! Will you tell them I can come to you whenever I like. Here's Mr. Molière forbidding me to enter your door—I, who opened it for him—the ingrate.

MOLIÈRE

Sire, have the goodness to tell the Duke that I am not an ingrate that I am only executing the orders given me.

D'ANJOU

All the same, I'm coming in.

KING

Go, Henriette, go.

(She leaves.)

D'ANJOU

(with a great sigh)

Ah.

KING

What's the matter with you, Anjou? You seem almost as sad as I am!

D'ANJOU

If I am sad, Louis, it's not for nothing.

KING

You, sad? Sad with 3,000 pounds in your pockets—that is to say with feathers in your cap, lace on your sleeves, diamond buckles on your gaiters, with gold braid on your cape?

D'ANJOU

Alas, exactly—it's because I must say goodbye to gold braid, to diamonds, to lace, to feathers, that I am sad! The three thousand crowns Mazarin gave me, you know?

KING

Yes.

D'ANJOU

Well, they're back in his vaults!

KING

He too them back?

D'ANJOU

No—he acted less honorably—he won them back from me gambling and when I was ruined, when my pocket was widowed of her last sou, when I wanted to play on honor he said to me, "Fie, Milord, how ugly it is to be a gambler at your age!" So you can see.

(turns out his pockets)

KING

And you are counting on me?

D'ANJOU

To fill their emptiness. I offered you yesterday your share of my three thousand crowns—today I came to ask you my share of your million—it's all the simple.

KING

Poor d'Anjou—you have bad luck.

D'ANJOU

Right—the Cardinal swindled you out of your million—too?

KING

No—but I've disposed of it.

D'ANJOU

Oh—and when will he give you another?

KING

I don't know—but don't worry—if he's too slow about it, I'll take it without asking him.

D'ANJOU

You are going to become King?

KING

I hope so.

D'ANJOU

Starting when?

KING

(with a sigh)

Starting today.

D'ANJOU

No one knows yet?

KING

No.

D'ANJOU

Well, let me be the first to pay you my compliment, Sire, I have the Honor—

(Molière scratches at he door.)

KING

Enter.

MOLIÈRE

The King will excuse me, but the Countess de Verceil and her daughter are leaving at noon and the King having given an audience to Miss Charlotte.

KING

Let her enter!

D'ANJOU

Who is this Miss Charlotte?

(Molière introduced Miss Charlotte, who remains shyly at the door)

Ah, it's the Maid of Honor to my cousin, Marguerite—say Louis, as soon as you touch that million—right?

KING

(offering him his hand)

Don't worry—I'll give you your three thousand.

D'ANJOU

Thanks—oh—nice ring!

KING

(sadly)

Here, take it.

D'ANJOU

For me?

KING

Yes—it will remind you that you were the first to congratulate me on my royal future.

D'ANJOU

Oh! What a pretty ring! Pretty ring! Thanks, Louis.

(as he passes Charlotte)

Here look—pretty ring—

CHARLOTTE

(still uncomfortable, ill at east)

Yes, Milord.

(Exit Anjou.)

KING

Lucky Anjou! A ring given, three thousand crowns promised and he's the happiest prince on earth.

(to Charlotte)

Come, miss.

CHARLOTTE

Pardon, Sire, it's a mistake, isn't it? In telling me, Your Majesty did me the honor of granting me an audience?

KING

What makes you suppose it is a mistake?

CHARLOTTE

Why that—why what, as for me, I have nothing to say to Your Majesty—no, nothing.

KING

But suppose the King has something to say to you?

CHARLOTTE

To me? What can the King have to say to me?

KING

He may have to ask you news of Princess Marguerite and her mother.

CHARLOTTE

They are very well, Sire, very well.

KING

The Regent is leaving at noon as they assure me?

CHARLOTTE

Yes, Sire.

KING

She's returning to Turin?

CHARLOTTE

Yes, to Turin.

KING

And what impression has this departure produced on her?

CHARLOTTE

She is very sad.

KING

In exchange, Princess Marguerite must be very gay.

CHARLOTTE

Very gay?

KING

Yes, isn't that the effect produced on her yesterday when the Queen Mother went up to the ladies quite furious, over the news of the love the King confessed to Miss Mancini.

CHARLOTTE

(aside)

My own words.

KING

And this gaiety is understandable, because she was afraid of marrying a man she didn't love—

CHARLOTTE

Oh!

KING

She's going to see Don Ranuce, Prince Farnese again!

CHARLOTTE

Oh!

KING

Who she loves tenderly.

CHARLOTTE

Oh.

KING

And who promised a certain Maid of Honor named Charlotte Godefroy—

CHARLOTTE

My God!

KING

Who for her part loves the Vicomte de Bouchavannes.

CHARLOTTE

My God—

KING

A hundred thousand pounds as a wedding gift if he were to marry Princess Marguerite.

CHARLOTTE

My God! Help! Help! I am going to be ill.

KING

You would do better to summon up all your strength and go take from that table you see there that paper folded in fours.

CHARLOTTE

Sire, it would be great pleasure—but my legs fail me—

KING

It's the Vicomte de Bouchavannes' commission as Captain.

CHARLOTTE

His commission as Captain? Oh, Sire—how to tank you—
Pardon, Sire!

KING

But you will give it to him, only on the condition—easily satisfied, that he will be your husband in six weeks—and now I have
only one more thing to tell you—if the Duke Farnese, whom
I am sparing a very expensive trip to France by not marrying
Princess Marguerite, is tight fisted enough not to give you that
hundred thousand pounds, I will give them to you.

CHARLOTTE

Oh, Sire.

KING

Well, what's the matter with you?

CHARLOTTE

Sire, fear, emotion, joy are producing such an effect on me that
I cannot see the door.

(he escorts her to the door)

But how could you know—?

KING

Allow me to return a kiss that you gave me last night at the foot of the turret stairs in Orangery Court—I do not want to have anything of Mr. de Bouchavannes'.

CHARLOTTE

Ah! My God.

(The door opens; Mazarin appears; Charlotte recoils. Mazarin takes a few steps forward. She scurries out behind him, head in her hands continuing to say.)

CHARLOTTE

My God! My God!

KING

(to himself)

Two happy, so far. For a moment, I almost forgot my misfortune.

MAZARIN

It's that, as Your Majesty begged me to stop by—I feared—

KING

(with hauteur)

I begged you to drop by, sir, because I have to discuss with you several important matters relative to the government of the kingdom and to our external and internal politics.

MAZARIN

Huh, Sire?

KING

Yes, that astonishes you, doesn't it, Cardinal Mazarin—that I am speaking to you in this manner? But there are some things which touch so closely my prerogatives as king or my feelings as a man that I am still astonished that you are accomplishing such matters without consulting me.

MAZARIN

Your Majesty, means—?

KING

I mean, sir—the refusal you gave to Mr. Condé to return to France and the order you gave my cousin, Charles, to leave Vincennes.

MAZARIN

Your Majesty knows—

KING

I know that Guenaud left yesterday evening for Brussels, and that King Charles was informed by Guitaut to leave Vincennes this morning.

MAZARIN

Oh! Oh!

KING

Why wasn't I informed of this, sir? It was less difficult to know, you will admit yourself, than the exact amount of your fortune! You know—I mean these 39 million 250 thousand pounds.

MAZARIN

Why of course, Sire! I am too clever a man not to give cleverness it's due. But, as the King seems to me to make a crime of the refusal to Prince Condé and the departure order given to His Majesty Charles II, I am going to try to justify myself briefly.

KING

Do so, sir, leave it to me to change the word justification to that of explanation.

MAZARIN

First of all, Sire, I didn't refuse Condé the right to return to France—I postponed it.

KING

Yes, to the end of his convalescence—and you fixed the term of that convalescence as two months.

MAZARIN

Sire, I am confident of people I employ; consequently you didn't learn what happened either from Bernouin or Guenaud nor from anyone of my house—you've learned it by chance! But the important thing is you know it. Well, I've kept Prince Condé out of France, because while doing justice to his great abilities as a general, I know his character as a politician. Prince Condé once at court instead of being with the army, no longer having any battles to win, Prince Condé will intrigue, maybe for Your Majesty may be against Your Majesty. He wants to marry you, not according to your tastes or the exigencies of politics, but according to his desires and interests. Then, so long as the King is not married or has not made an irrevocable choice for his marriage, I prefer that Prince Condé be in Brussels rather than Paris.

KING

On that point, I grant you are right—and I promise you that before Prince Condé is in Paris I have made an irrevocable choice.

MAZARIN

Then they will no longer be any obstacle and Guenaud will cure the Prince and Your Majesty will recall him as swiftly as God and the King (my only two lords in heaven and earth) permit.

KING

Let's pass to King Charles II.

MAZARIN

Ah, as to King Charles, that's another matter and Your Majesty will, shortly agree with me that his presence in Vincennes, in Paris and even in France was impossible.

KING

You will admit all the same sir, that it is permitted for me, myself a fugitive and proscribed once as he is, to ask you for an explanation of this order given by a minister to a King to leave the country of his cousin and his ally as if he were only a simple private person.

MAZARIN

First of all, my dear, Sire—a dispossessed King is at the same time less and more than a simple private person—because he is sometimes troublesome, never useful, and always dangerous. Then, King Charles is your cousin, it's true; but in saying he is your ally, you are mistaken; your ally, Sire, is Mr. Richard Cromwell, Protector of Great Britain. Still, if your cousin is proscribed and a fugitive as you once were, it's because he had the misfortune of not having by him a Jules Mazarin as you had. But for that, instead of traveling the great highways, he would at this hour be on the throne of England.

KING

I know all that I owe you, sir, and be sure I will never forget it. I do justice to your genius to which I recognize I owe the peace, my throne and my power—but that genius, however great it may be can ill judge a situation or make an error. I am allied to Mr. Richard Cromwell? Me? I was unaware of that. The treaty of alliance with the new Lord Protector was approved by you on my behalf? Then, it's true, for your action as minister engages the King of France who was so weak or forgetful to leave such an act to his minister.

MAZARIN

Sire, I've been practicing politics for thirty years—with Cardinal Zinneti first, then Cardinal Richelieu, then finally, all alone—I did it with passion, with flair—I had one passion in my youth—flair still—I can indeed say, since it's the greatest reproach against me—well, Sir, this politics, I must confess has not always been very honest, but it has never been clumsy—so that it follows that for me to put King Charles on the throne would be at once clumsy and dishonest, Sire!

KING

Dishonest!

MAZARIN

Yes, since you concluded a treaty with Oliver Cromwell—the father—

KING

And even, in that treaty—he signed above me—he put his name higher than mine.

MAZARIN

Eh! Sire, it's Your Majesty's fault, why did you sign so low? Eh! My God, Mr. Cromwell found a good place, he took it, it was his habit, you know.

KING

Yes, but as I was saying, now Oliver Cromwell is dead.

MAZARIN

Right! Do you think that because he is buried, the King is dead, long live the King? Oliver Cromwell is dead but Richard Cromwell is his father's heir and has succeeded him—the treaty you signed with the father—that treaty is more valuable than ever! At bottom was it unsound? No! A man dies, is buried, placed in a shroud—it's the form that is shrouded, buried, dead—the principal lives. Ah, My God! I know indeed that it's disloyal from the point of view of the family to sign a treaty with a man who cut the throat of our uncle—and from the moral point of view—to have contracted an alliance with a Parliament called the Rump—but it wasn't clumsy from the political viewpoint, while our coffers were empty, Oliver Cromwell loaned me five millions and at a time when I had no army, sent me five thousand Scotsmen—with those troops I saved France from a foreign war it was in no condition to undertake—with the money I kept alive Your Majesty and his august family that, without the money, would have died of starvation—with the troops I repressed the revolt—! You see indeed, he did good sometimes—this dear Oliver Cromwell— Holland is protecting King Charles—to whom I wish all sorts of prosperity—let Holland do it, where I am sending him back. Thanks to that return it will squabble with England. England and Holland squabble—they will fight each other—they are the only two naval powers in Europe let them fight each other—let them destroy each others navies—and we will build our fleet from the debris of their ships—if I find a way by economizing enough money to buy the nails.

KING

It seems to me, sir, that the moment has come—thanks to those thirty-nine million two hundred and sixty thousand pounds.

MAZARIN

First of all, Sire, there's no more than thirty-eight million two hundred and sixty thousand pounds, since yesterday, I gave a million to Your Majesty. Then Sire, those thirty-eight million two hundred sixty thousand pounds no longer belong to me, and it may be, when the hour we are speaking of arrives that I will be dead, and that my heir who I think is a bit of a prodigal— may have spent them.

KING

You've disposed of these thirty-eight millions by will? And in whose favor, sir?

MAZARIN

In favor of the one in whose service I have earned them, Sire—here, would you cast a glance at this will; it wasn't made just yesterday, since it is written by Mr. Colbert, my first clerk, who's been in Lyons for the last two months.

KING

(after having read it)

What me—your only heir—your residual legatee? It's to me you wish to leave your fortune?

MAZARIN

Isn't this money yours? Isn't it in your service that I earned it? Poor I came to the land of France, I have nothing to ask of France except a tomb for my body and in that tomb—eternal repose.

KING

But your family, Mr. Mazarin?

MAZARIN

I have only nephews and nieces, and sometimes Your Majesty has done me the honor of calling me his father—besides I know Your Majesty's heart—Your Majesty will not leave in misery the relatives of a good servant who spent all his life in your service and that of France.

KING

(looking at him with astonishment)

OH!

(a moment of silence)

Well, listen Monsieur Mazarin, as minister and as father I am going to consult you on the most important action of my life. Monsieur Mazarin, I love your niece, Miss Mancini.

MAZARIN

Ah! My King, my dear King!

KING

I love her to the point of making her my wife, if you will indeed grant her to me.

MAZARIN

Sire! Sire! That's too much honor for the son of a poor fisherman from Pissina—to become the father-in-law of a King—but still if you demand it, my duty is to obey you.

KING

Yes, but I told you I wanted your advice, having a choice to make between a woman I love and a princess I have never seen—and who, consequently is indifferent to me. Ought I to marry the woman I love, that is to say, Marie Mancini or the princess who is indifferent to me—that is to say—the Infanta of Spain?

MAZARIN

(very agitated)

But the Infanta, Sire, the Infanta—you can only marry her if Her Majesty, the Queen of Spain, gives birth to a boy.

KING

The Queen of Spain has given birth to a boy.

MAZARIN

Are you quite sure of that, Sire—? How can you know that if I don't know?

KING

You would have known that last night, if Signor Pimentel, the Spanish Ambassador instead of going to join you in the Orangery where you were waiting for him hadn't been escorted directly to me.

MAZARIN

By whom, Sire?

KING

By me, myself, sir.

MAZARIN

A boy! A boy! Terrible news!

KING

Here's the letter from the King notifying us of the birth of a boy baptized under the name Charles.

MAZARIN

That doesn't say that the King of Spain will grant us the Infanta.

KING

Here's the letter from Philip IV which offers her to me. Now, sir—who ought I to marry? Marie Mancini or the Infanta?

MAZARIN

Sire! Ah, Mazarin! Poor Marazin! Sire! Sire!

(falling on his knees)

The glory of my king and the grandeur of France before all else!

Sire, with despair in my heart, but conviction in my soul—I tell you—marry the Infanta!

KING

You tell me this?

MAZARIN

Yes, and if I told you anything else, my King, you must not believe me—you must tell me, "No, sir, no! You are an egoist, ambitious, a bad minister."

KING

So you insist?

MAZARIN

Oh, my dear King, be great! Be greater than the predecessors of Your Majesty and let posterity say: "A portion of this greatness the King received from the son of a poor fisherman from Pissina" and Mazarin. Mazarin—well, he will be rewarded for his thirty years of devotion to your father and you—

(Anne of Austria appears in the doorway.)

KING

It's not at my feet you must tell me this, sir, its' in my arms, it's in my heart.

MAZARIN

Oh, Sire, Sire! Thanks for the great honor that you do me.

KING

My mother.

MAZARIN

The Queen!

KING

Silence, sir, I am awaiting your niece here.

MAZARIN

Sire, I go to obey Your Majesty's orders.

(Exit Mazarin.)

ANNE

(aside)

The Cardinal in the arms of the King—the King expecting the Cardinal's niece—it's all over, decided, accomplished, and I've come too late. No matter.

(to the King who comes to her after having escorted the Cardinal)

Sire—

KING

Mother?

ANNE

It seems you've just announced a great and joyous news to His Eminence.

KING

Yes, Madame—a news that completes all his wishes and satisfies all mine.

ANNE

(with bitterness)

News relative to your marriage, doubtless?

KING

Your customary sagacity hasn't misled you, mother.

ANNE

Then everything is settled—you've chosen a wife for yourself and a Queen for France.

KING

Yes, Madame.

ANNE

You'd made that choice without consulting me?

KING

When my choice is known I hope my mother will approve it.

ANNE

And if by chance, it were otherwise. That choice, if I condemned it, if I declared it impolitic, anti-royal, impossible?

KING

That would be a misfortune, Madame, but it wouldn't change my decision.

ANNE

So that decision is irrevocable?

KING

Irrevocable, Madame.

ANNE

Then you are declaring war on me—? It's a battle you are under-
taking against your mother?

KING

I beg you to keep your tenderness for me—I demand your
blessing.

ANNE

My blessing! My tenderness—when you prick me at the same
time in my mother's love and my queenly pride? Oh, no Sire,
you mustn't count on it.

KING

And what must I expect, Madame?

ANNE

To find in me the most relentless opponent of this union! And
from this moment, I tell you sir, my precautions are taken.

KING

(teeth closed in rage)

Your precautions? Listen carefully, Madame, it may be, when I
am dead, when I am sleeping at Saint Denis, in the vault of my
ancestors, in the sepulcher of my predecessors, when I am no

longer around, whip, sword or scepter in hand to say "That's what I want"—they can upset my desires, they can break my will, they can destroy what I have done—but so long as I'm living, in control, reigning, all will bow, all will yield, and all will bend under my will!

ANNE

Even—?

KING

Even my ministers! Even my mother! Even destiny!

ANNE

Oh, Louis, Louis, what's made you like this?

KING

The knowledge of the truth, Madame! The truth that is kept so carefully from kings—that I've called to me, that I lean on.

ANNE

(tenderly)

Louis.

KING

Mother, perhaps instead of great sadness, great joy is reserved for you—go into this room. Soon my court will come here to learn the news of my marriage and the name of the woman I've chosen—you will come take your place at my side. Cardinal Mazarin will take his at my left—and I tell you—at the announcement of this marriage, of the name of the woman he will marry—you will bless your son instead of cursing him— Go, mother! I am expecting Miss Mancini and you mustn't be found here with her.

ANNE

Miss Mancini?

KING

Yes, mother.

ANNE

Do whatever you wish, but—

KING

No threats, Madame.

(The King kisses her hand. She enters the next room.)

KING

(alone)

Come, my heart, temper yourself like steel, purify yourself like diamond.

MOLIÈRE

(enter Marie, introduced by Molière)

Enter miss—the King is expecting you.

MARIE

Sire! Sire! What my uncle told me? It's impossible isn't it?

KING

What did he tell you, Marie?

MARIE

He told me to quit the court this very day, that I am to leave with my sister, Hortense, that I must enshroud myself in the depths of Saintonge—oh, Sire, what did you tell me? What did you promise me? What was this future to which you opened my eyes? What has become of this splendid path down which you made me take some steps—side by side with you—leaning on your arm? Where is this dazzling end you showed me? Why make a poor mortal see a half opened heaven? Why call her your friend, your lover, your queen, only to de-crown her—of the only crown she was ambitious to attain—that of your love—

KING

Alas, yes, Marie, you've just made the story of your life and it is indeed, what I too have dreamed—but what do you expect? Every novel has its ending—every dream its awakening—what we had hoped for yesterday is impossible today—

MARIE

Impossible! And this a loving heart, a royal heart which says this to me! But to attain the goal you proposed to me; to me, I who am only a woman, having neither power, nor riches, nor majesty—for me nothing is impossible! Oh, nothing—I swear to you, no nothing! What was possible yesterday is not possible today? Then what's happened? Between that sweet and charming storm in the forest, during which you told me you loved me—and this calm—so full of lightning for me—and flashes where you tell me that you no longer love me—what insurmountable obstacle has arisen?

KING

What obstacle has arisen, Marie? I am going to tell you—a breath has passed over the mirror of our love and tarnished it; a stone has been thrown into the limpid lake where we were searching for that little pearl called happiness and—disturbed it. Oh, for a virginal heart, for a love entirely mine—Marie, God is my witness to all I've struggled against and with the help of God and the divine power in me, I would have triumphed over everything.

MARIE

But is this divine flame extinguished?

KING

Alas, you yourself blew it out, Marie!

MARIE

Oh, I don't understand.

KING

Recall in all its details the night which just slipped by—where were you a little after midnight? For whom did you open the window of your room which gives on the court of the Orangery? Who were you waiting for at that window—and who approached it? Who spoke a quarter of an hour with you—to whom did you return his letters—of whom did you ask yours back?

MARIE

Oh! My God.

KING

De Guiche, right?

MARIE

Unfortunate me! Yes, I don't deny it—from de Guiche.

KING

No, Marie, no—you are mistaken, it wasn't de Guiche, it was me. Me! Me! Ah, you are suffering you say? Suffer—suffer, Marie—and you will never suffer as much as I have suffered.

MARIE

Why, if it was you, Sire, you must have understood, must have understood all that I said. You know nothing staining my honor escaped my mouth. Poor, isolated, abandoned since my childhood, by my sisters, older and more beautiful than I, I was waiting my turn to enter life, asking as a flower does, only some air and sunshine—; I turned to Mr. Guiche's voice, on the side of love—I loved him—or I thought I loved him—it's true, but the one for whom I broke with de Guiche, the one that I truly loved—and of that love, I was certain for it was sacred through my tears—the one I truly loved—is you, Sire—! It's you alone—the one I will always love—is you—why must there be a change in the heaven of our love because a cloud passed over it last night—which dawn will blow away with the wind.

KING

Yes, Marie, but that cloud was observed, seen, recognized by others beside me, that cloud makes a stain on the sun of royalty. Caesar repudiated his wife on a suspicion—for the wife of Caesar must not even be suspected.

MARIE

Oh, yes; but Caesar didn't love his wife, and you love me; Caesar didn't weep when he left her and you are weeping.

(she pulls his hand from his face)

See for himself!

KING

Oh! Marie! Marie!

MARIE

You are king, you will weep and I will leave—oh!

KING

Marie—here are you letters that you asked for back from de Guiche.

MARIE

That's fine. Everything is over, Sire, but before leaving you forever—

KING

Forever, yes.

MARIE

Let me tell you one thing. You are sacrificing me—not to your jealousy—on, you know quite well, Sire—that this love for Mr. Guiche was only a child's dream on my part—only this dream serves you as a pretext—you are sacrificing me not to your jealousy but to that cruel divinity of Kings called reason of State—you push me out of your heart not because I love another, you know quite well it is you I love—but because I am not the daughter nor the sister of a king.

KING

Marie!

MARIE

Oh, hear me, these are my last words—it's my last testament of love—you believe you must act this way and you are not disturbed over the wrong you are doing to a poor soul who never harmed you—well, by this decision you are making, you are outraging, Sire, another divinity no less powerful, but for sure more immutable than "Reason of State"—it's human reason which says to every heart, "seek a heart, and unite with one that loves you!" Well, Sire, this heart that man searched for without consulting the King—that heart which he found—was mine—

KING

Marie.

MARIE

Oh! I have no more words to say and I leave you, quit you, obey you—but in obeying you—I leave you to a woman you've never seen and that you don't love—from whom you will demand love—and she will offer you only submission! then—then— the poor Marie you had loved so much and who had been so happy to love you—you will need—you will look around you; she won't be there anymore—then this joy that your wife will refuse you—sorry—your queen—you will seek in other loves. You will fritter away your heart on twenty mistresses. What will you demand of them—these mistresses that you will leave one after another? Marie! Marie! Always Marie! But Marie will no longer be there—Marie will be far away—Marie will be ruined—Marie will be dead or mad—goodbye, Sire—be happy—now, if God will permit it—

(At the moment of leaving, she stops to cast one last glance at the King—who despite himself has taken a step towards her, seeing the King turn away his eyes, she rushes from the apartment with a gesture of despair. The King falls into an armchair and rests his head in his two hands. Molière enters and remains standing before the king—a moment of silence where only the King's breathing can be heard—little by little he raises his head, then notices Molière.)

KING

What are you doing there, sir?

MOLIÈRE

Sire, I am assisting at the most sublime spectacle a poet is allowed to contemplate—the struggle of a man against human passions.

KING

You are mistaken, sir, it's not the man that you are contemplating, it's the King. A man would have given way to his passions—the King conquered them! Here, look—look at me.

(smiling sadly)

The will can do whatever it wants. I want to forget. What happened did not exist. Marie Mancini what do you mean, sir? I never knew a woman by that name—she who left his room is a hundred leagues from here already—or rather wasn't here—! Good—we are at the end of our comedy, Mr. Molière

As I told you this morning the reversal is accomplished all that remains is the denouement. let's see what remains for me to do, and what scene am I in—? Ah, I remember Mr. Molière one must have it all prepared in the armoire—set it in this little table.

MOLIÈRE

I am then still Valet de Chambre to Your Majesty?

KING

Yes, for an instant, still—place two covers—I have a guest—on the napkin of the guest place this paper.

MOLIÈRE

Sire!

(Georgette enters with a plate of fruits in her hand.)

KING

Who's entering! Ah! It's Georgette.

GEORGETTE

Good! this falls out well! My father told me—"Go pick the most
beautiful fruits of the orchard little one—and bring them to the
King for his lunch." I arrive just as the King is going to set at
the table.

KING

Oh you, you always arrive at the right time, Georgette.

GEORGETTE

The King is happy with his, right?

KING

Yes, Georgette.

GEORGETTE

Things happened as the King desired?

KING

Couldn't be better.

GEORGETTE

And did the King learn what he desired to know?

KING

Everything—and even more.

MOLIÈRE

Sire, the table is ready.

KING

That's fine. Sit down there, Molière.

MOLIÈRE

Me, at this table?

KING

At that table, yes.

MOLIÈRE

My duty is to obey—but Your Majesty—

KING

As for me, I am sitting here.

MOLIÈRE

(taking the paper on his napkin)

Sire.

KING

Read that paper, Molière—isn't it for my guest?

MOLIÈRE

(after having glanced at the paper)

The license I solicited of Your Majesty—that privilege is granted to me—

KING

Yes, but on one condition.

MOLIÈRE

Which is?

KING

You will engage in your turn a young actress that I recommend to you.

MOLIÈRE

And where is she, Sire?

KING

Here she is.

MOLIÈRE

Georgette?

GEORGETTE

Yes, me, Mr. Molière—and you will see how well I will work indeed—! You will see that I have talent! Thanks, Sire! Thanks! Oh, what luck! What luck!

POQUELIN

(appearing at the door. Molière has his back turned, searching in his pockets)

Sire—excuse me, Sire.

MOLIÈRE

Good! My father! I informed Your Majesty earlier—

KING

Ah! There are you, Mr. Poquelin! What do you want?

POQUELIN

Sire! I am going to ask you first of all, if, in the petition that I had the honor to remit to Your Majesty—there had slipped.

KING

Yes, a paper, right? A paper on which is a bill to pay 20,000 pounds signed by Mazarin?

POQUELIN

That's exactly correct, sir! I thought I'd lost it—since yesterday I've been searching everywhere, turned my pockets inside out—

KING

Here, Mr. Poquelin in that billfold there on the console.

POQUELIN

Thanks, Sire, now it remains for me to beg Your Majesty to do right by my request and grant me the letter de cachet solicited by me to have my rascally son imprisoned who—who—

(stupefied, he recognizes his son)

My son at table with the King.

KING

Mr. Molière, may I offer you a wing of this partridge?

POQUELIN

Oh! My God! My God!

KING

Mr. Poquelin—introduce all the persons who are waiting in the antechamber.

MOLIÈRE

(wishing to rise)

Sire!

KING

No, stay.

POQUELIN

(opening the doors at the back)

Enter, gentlemen, enter, gentlemen, enter, gentlemen!

KING

Georgette, open this door and go tell Queen Anne, on my behalf, who's made you so frightened that she can come in.

(Georgette obeys.)

(All the characters enter except Guenaud; the courtiers are astonished—there's whispering.)

DANGEAU

Well, it appears I was not mistaken and that the secret agent was indeed Molière.

MONTGLAT

You are witness that I refused to name him, but since the King himself reveals him—

CHARLOTTE

But I thought he was lunching this morning with you—

MONTGLAT

He had promised me to but he told me a quarter of an hour ago that it was impossible for him to keep his promise since he was lunching with the King.

KING

Gentleman, you see me sharing my lunch with Molière, who Bontemps, my valet de chambre didn't find worthy of making my bed.

MONTGLAT

Sire, His Majesty Louis XIII issued a decree declaring that the acting profession could not be considered blameworthy.

KING

And I am implementing that edict as you see, sir.

(He rises, Molière rises, too—taking the table with him— Montglat, Villequier, Dangeau rush to help him saying—Mr. Molière, Mr. Molière.)

KING

(aside)

A valet refused to make my bed with an actor and there are Dukes and Peers who help that actor to buss my table. O Molière! Molière—why do you insist on leaving the court.

(aloud)

Gentlemen, the King has brought you together to announce to you that through the good works of his mother, Anne of Austria, to whom he will be eternally grateful, and through the able negotiations of Cardinal Mazarin, who he will never be rich enough or powerful enough to adequately reward—he's going to marry the Infanta of Spain—Marie Theresa.

ALL

Oh! Sire—Your Majesty—The Infanta.

ANNE

My King.

KING

Say: 'My Son,' Madame.

MAZARIN

(passing a paper to the King)

Here, Sire!

KING

(in a low voice)

Thanks—father!

(aloud)

And here is the authority that I give to Cardinal Mazarin to represent me and to represent France at the conferences which will have to take place to conclude my marriage with The Infanta and peace with Spain.

(going to a table and singing it)

'Louis, King—

GRAMMONT

King! And since when?

GUITAUT

Since this morning; an hour ago.

DANGEAU

(on the fringe, near Molière, writing in his notebook)

"The King's secret agent was Molière."

MOLIÈRE

(hearing him)

That's how they write history!

CURTAIN

ABOUT THE AUTHOR

Frank J. Morlock has written and translated many plays since retiring from the legal profession in 1992. His translations have also appeared on Project Gutenberg, the Alexandre Dumas Père web page, Literature in the Age of Napoléon, Infinite Artistries.com, and Munsey's (formerly Blackmask). In 2006 he received an award from the North American Jules Verne Society for his translations of Verne's plays. He lives and works in México.

www.ingramcontent.com/pod-product-compliance
Lightning Source LLC
Chambersburg PA
CBHW031945090426
42739CB00006B/85